So, You Think You Know Martha's Vineyard?

People, Places, Folklore, Trivia
and Treasures

By Melissa Bigelow

Omni Publishing Co.
2023

Published by Omni Publishing Co.
www.omni-pub.com

Cover Design: Dave Derby
www.DerbyCreative.com

Library of Congress cataloging in publication data
Bigelow, Melissa

So, You Think You Know Martha's Vineyard?
People, Places, Folklore, Trivia and Treasures

ISBN: 978-1-928758-10-5

Preface

Martha's Vineyard is an iconic Massachusetts island, known for its beautiful beaches, charming villages, and unique culture. With a rich history dating back to the Wampanoag Tribe who first inhabited it in the 17th century, Martha's Vineyard has since become a popular vacation destination for people from all over the world. In this book, we will explore everything that makes Martha's Vineyard so special - from its stunning beaches and landscapes to its vibrant tourist industry. We will also discover some of the most interesting stories behind famous landmarks, hidden gems and secret beaches on the island.

The people of Martha's Vineyard have strong ties to their community, working together to make it a better place for all. From small businesses to philanthropic organizations, this tight-knit group works tirelessly to ensure everyone can enjoy the island's natural beauty and cultural heritage.

The sense of camaraderie extends beyond the island as well - with people from around the world visiting each year in search of adventure or relaxation. Here they will find an inviting atmosphere filled with enthusiastic locals eager to share stories of their beloved island home.

So if you're looking to get away from it all and experience something truly unique, then come along with us as we take a journey through the wonderful world of Martha's Vineyard!

Author Information

Melissa K. Bigelow, a Magna Cum Laude graduate of Boston University and CERTIFIED FINANCIAL PLANNER™, is a resident of Mashpee, MA. She is a native Cape Codder, born at Cape Cod Hospital and raised in Yarmouth. She worked in banking and finance for 12 years, ten of which were spent at a local mutual savings bank and the last two at a national financial services firm. She is currently the owner of Seagull Treasure Chest, an online retail establishment specializing in pre-1900 antique books. The business, which she operates out of her home in Mashpee, is in memory of her late father, Tom Hague's, brick and mortar antique store of the same name, which he operated during the 1970s in West Harwich.

Her life's greatest accomplishment is her twelve-year old daughter, Sophia, a frequent high honors student who plays tennis and soccer for the Monomoy Regional School District. You can catch Sophia on stage during the summer at one of Cape Cod Theatre Company's musical productions.

A lifelong writer, Melissa's dream as a child was to become an author. This is her second book and the fourth in a series published by Henry M. Quinlan, the owner and publisher of Omni Publishing Company. The first and second books in the series are *So, You Think You Know the South Coast?*; *So, You Think You Know Cape Cod?; and So, You Think You Know Nantucket?*

Table of Contents

Martha's Vineyard

In 1602, English explorer and privateer, **Bartholomew Gosnold**, led an expedition to the eastern coast of North America on the *Concord*. On May 21st, he spotted an island off the coast of Cape Cod. Gabriel Archer, a crew member aboard the vessel, wrote in his journal, *"...coasting along we saw a disinhabited island, which so afterward appeared unto us: we bore with it, and named it Martha's Vineyard."* Gosnold named the island after his firstborn daughter, who died in infancy in 1598, and the wild grapes that grew in abundance on the island. Gosnold described Martha's Vineyard as 'most pleasant' in his log, noting the abundance of woods, vines, raspberries, deer, and an assortment of shore and seabirds as they explored the island on May 22nd.

Martha's Vineyard is located in Duke's County, which encompasses 11 islands off the coast of Southeastern Massachusetts. The Vineyard is the largest island, both in area and population, with 99% of the county's population residing there. Nine islands in the county constitute the Elizabeth island chains: Nonamesset, Uncatena, Weepecket, Gull, Naushon, Pasque, Nashawena, Penekise and Cuttyhunk. Penekise and Cuttyhunk are open to the public; the remainder of the islands are privately owned by the Forbes family. The aptly named No Man's Land is an uninhabited isle off the southwest end of Martha's Vineyard, and the 11th island in the county.

The Vineyard comprises six towns: **Aquinnah, Chilmark, Edgartown, Oak Bluffs, Vineyard Haven, and West Tisbury**. Chappaquiddick Island, known as "Chappy," is a small peninsula that is part of Edgartown and occasionally separated from the mainland during storms and hurricanes.

Geographically, Martha's Vineyard sits in the Atlantic Ocean, six miles off the coast of Cape Cod and thirty seven miles from Nantucket. Ferries and planes provide transportation between both islands and the mainland. At 96 square miles with 124 miles of coastline, it is more than double the area of Nantucket. Long considered a tourist colony, its year round population has swelled over the years, and in 2020, permanent dwellings outnumbered seasonal units for the first time in five decades.

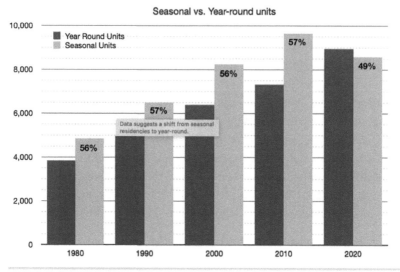

Data suggests a shift from seasonal residencies to year-round.

Source: The Vineyard Gazette "Census Shows Vineyard Population

Has Grown, Diversified" August 19, 2021

The year round population of 20,600 balloons to nearly 200,000 in the summer, 63% of whom own seasonal residences. Similar to other areas across the United States, Martha's Vineyard is becoming more diverse, with non-white populations growing at a much faster rate than their white counterparts. African Americans, Latinos, and American Indians have increased in number in all towns except Aquinnah. The island also boasts a large Brazilian population, and Portuguese is recognized as the second most widely spoken language in the area.

The median age of year round residents is 53.9 and the average income is about $132,000, with three quarters of residents classified as white collar workers, and the remainder as blue collar. The four key industries that make up more than half of the island's economy are hospitality, retail, construction, and real estate. The island's status as a summer colony with seasonal residents and visitors is what drives a large percentage of economic activity.

People of Significance

Governor Thomas Mayhew (March 31, 1593 – March 25, 1682) established the first European settlement on Martha's Vineyard, Nantucket and adjacent islands in 1642. He is one of the editors of the Bay Psalm Book, the first book published in the Thirteen Colonies. His assistant Peter Foulger was the grandfather of Benjamin Franklin. With the help of his son Thomas, a settlement was established and farming and whaling enterprises were begun.

The Mayhews had great success regarding Indian policy and due to the fair treatment of the Indians there, the colony was protected from the bloodshed that occurred elsewhere during King Philip's War. Native American literacy in the schools founded by Thomas Mayhew Jr. and taught by Peter Folger was such that the first Native American graduates of Harvard were from Martha's Vineyard.

Mayhew's successor as leader of the community was the **Hon. Leavitt Thaxter**. He married Martha Mayhew, a descendant of Thomas Mayhew, and was an Edgartown educator described by Indian Commissioner John Milton Earle as "a long and steadfast friend to the Indians." After living in Northampton, Thaxter, a lawyer, returned home to Edgartown, where he took over the school founded by his father, Rev. Joseph Thaxter. He also served in the State House and the Senate, was a member of the Massachusetts Governor's Council and later served as US Customs Collector for Martha's Vineyard.

Having rechristened his father's Edgartown school Thaxter Academy, Hon. Leavitt Thaxter was granted on February 15, 1845, the sum of $50-per-year for "the support of William Johnson, an Indian of the Chappequiddic tribe." By this time, Leavitt Thaxter had taken on the role, described in an act passed by the General Court of Massachusetts, as "guardian of the Indians and people of color resident at Chappequiddic and Indiantown in the County of Dukes County." Thaxter Academy, founded by Leavitt Thaxter as first principal in 1825, became known for educating both white and Native American youth.

One of the first houses built in what is now Oak Bluffs was built at Farm Neck by **Joseph Norton** before 1670. It stood near the half-way watering place on the highway that leads from Edgartown to Vineyard Haven. A description of this house will apply to nearly all the houses built at that time. With two or three exceptions they were of one story; large on the base and low in the post. They were always located near springs of fresh water, or where water could be had by digging shallow wells at which old-fashioned sweeps could be used.

Another interesting fact is that near the site of these ancient dwellings can be seen old pear and cherry trees, which tradition says were planted soon after these houses were built. The frames of these houses were of oak and pine which grew near. There was a saw pit in the neighborhood, to which these great trees, many of which were three feet in diameter, were hauled by oxen and sawed into convenient dimensions by hand, one man in the pit and another above.

All About Aquinnah

Aquinnah, located in the southwestern corner of Martha's Vineyard, is the smallest town on the island by population (439 people according to the 2020 census) and area (40.8 square miles). The town was incorporated as Gay Head in 1870, but officially changed its name to the Wampanoag name of Aquinnah in 1997 to represent recognition of the Wampanoag tribe in the area. To understand this community, it is important to go back to its earliest history, which begins with a legend.

Moshup was a mythical giant from Wampanoag folklore. One day, he was journeying across the mainland towards the cliffs of Aquinnah. Tired from his trek, he began to drag one of his feet, leaving a large track in the mud. Gradually, water began to fill his imprint, eventually creating the island, Noepe. The Wampanoag settled in Aquinnah, hunting and fishing across the entire island of Martha's Vineyard at least ten thousand years ago.

When English settlers arrived in 1669, they encroached upon the natives' land and designated the area from Nashaquitsa Pond in Chilmark to the Cliffs of Aquinnah as an Indian District. The colonists later divided Chilmark and Aquinnah into two separate towns, incorporating the latter as Gay Head, which described the beautiful red cliffs of the area. The Wampanoag objected to the town's incorporation, despite the settlers' offers of full citizenship and voting rights. Nevertheless, the majority of the population remained Wampanoag, and so they continued to control the town government for the next century.

To protect their interests, the **Wampanoag Tribe of Gay Head** was formed in 1972, eventually receiving federal recognition through the Bureau of Indian Affairs in 1987, and the ability to control tribal lands within the town's boundaries. The 485 acres of tribal lands consists of 160 acres of private land and 325 acres of common land, including the Gay Head cliffs, Herring Creek, and Lobsterville. In 1991, the town made a failed attempt to change the name back to Aquinnah, which means "land under the hill." It wasn't until 1997 that residents voted, and this time won by a narrow margin, officially changing the town's name.

Vineyard Sound is the northern border of the town, with the Atlantic Ocean to the south and west. It is one of the few western-facing coastlines of the eastern U.S. The town of Chilmark is its only land border to the east and is separated by Menemsha Bight, Menemsha Pond, and Squibnocket Pond. State Road, which runs between the two ponds, is the only road into Aquinnah. Its geography includes a rolling terrain of woodlands and high peaked sand dunes, and of course, its famous red cliffs. The clay cliffs, which are part of the Wampanoag common lands, were formed by the retreating Laurentide ice sheet approximately 18,000 years ago. They are environmentally protected to limit erosion.

Aquinnah has three public beaches. **Philbin Beach** off Moshup Trail has a resident only parking area that requires a parking pass year round, but the beach is open to the public. Situated at the base of the cliffs, it's an uncrowded beach with miles of shoreline that's known for its surf. Take in views of No Man's Land, Cuttyhunk, and other islands offshore.

Aquinnah Public Beach and **Moshup Beach** are also located off Moshup Trail. There is a paid parking area that's a ten minute walk from the beach; it's mostly downhill, but best to wear good footwear as opposed to flip flops. Stop by the cliffs overlook before heading down the trail to catch some spectacular views, especially at sunset. There is also a dropoff area closer to the beach. Crowds tend to be larger near the trailhead. Bathroom facilities are available, with accessible port-a-potties when the restrooms are closed. These beaches are also at the foot of the cliffs and feature miles of pristine shoreline. Moshup Beach, which is further west, is popular with nude sunbathers; there are no signs indicating this section of the beach, so be courteous if you venture down to this area. There are no lifeguards on duty at either beach so leave Fido at home since "no dogs" signs are posted.

Lobsterville Beach features two miles of Vineyard Sound shoreline on Lobsterville Road. The beach is free and open to the public, but parking is limited. Most of the spaces require a resident permit, but there are a few spots where anyone can park. Arrive early to ensure a spot. With little surf, this beach is especially popular with families with small children. Dogs are allowed here; in fact, it's the only beach that allows furry friends year round. It's also a popular spot for fishing, birdwatching, paddleboarding and kayaking.

There is a resident-only beach on Menemsha Pond called **Red Beach** or Head of the Pond. It features calm waters and is the perfect place to launch a kayak. West Basin is also located on Menemsha Pond at the end of Lobsterville Road. A resident permit is also required; however, Tribal members may park at the bend along West Basin Road to access common land that is a federally granted birthright for all members of the Wampanoag Tribe of Gay Head (Aquinnah).

People of Significance - Aquinnah

Ebenezer Skiff was the first lighthouse keeper of Gay Head Light, serving from 1799 to 1828. In December of 1804, he discovered an abandoned ship near the lighthouse. Not a soul was onboard, but the cargo hold was full. He posted a notice about it in the January 21, 1805 edition of the New York Gazette & General Advertiser.

> *Martba's Vineyard, Dec.* 31.—" Yefterday about noon drifted on fhore within a mile fouth of the light-houfe on Gay Head, a floop, maft broke off about the middle, boom and head of the maft overboard, tiller in the becket windward lanyard cut, fails hanging to leeward, no perfon, regifter, nor principal papers found on board at prefent. The laft date of reckoning found is Dec. 27, followed by other obfervations which probably were made. on the 28th. On a fmall piece of paper found in one of the chefts are thefe words, viz. Wm. Hawes fhipt on board of the floop Harmony, of Kingfton, Benjamin Hawes, mafter, bound to Baltimore, and from thence elfewhere and back to Bofton." By another paper it appears that in Bofton, Nov. 2. 1804, there were fhipt on board the floop Harmony, in the harbor of Bofton, bound to Baltimore, 16 bbls and 6 boxes, to be delivered to Oliver Fuller.— Found in a pocket-book a receipt for Cephas Wadfworth's taxes, dated Kingfton, Jan. 12. 1804, figned by Sylvanus Bradford, Collector. Said wreck's cargo chiefly confifts of Flour, fouthern Corn, and boxes or bales, fuppofed to be dry goods. Have with others taken out the boxes and put them into faid light-houfe—110 bbls. and fome corn are now on the beach under watch; fhall endeavour to fave and fecure as foon as may be —There is more cargo yet on board.— With the owners and thofe concerned to come with fuitable credentials, pay charges and fupercede in the care of the wreck and property. EBENEZER SKIFF, *Keeper of faid Light Houfe.*"

Amos Peter Smalley, a Wampanoag tribal member, was born in 1877 in Gay Head. He was a well-known whaler who first went to sea at age fifteen. In 1902, Amos set sail on the New Bedford based ship,

Platina. Off the coast of the Azores, a 90-foot white sperm whale was spotted. Amos boarded a small 30-foot whaleboat with a crew, and killed the great beast with a bomb lance, a type of harpoon with an exploding head.

Former Wampanoag historian and director of education for the Wampanoag Tribe of Gay Head, **Helen Manning**, who passed away in 2008, was Amos' niece. In 2000, she published the book, *Moshup's Footsteps*, and included her uncle's recollections about the great white whale. Amos recounted the story of the last great sachem (chief) of Aquinnah, Mittark, who, on his deathbed, warned of strangers coming to Aquinnah. As a sign of his prophecy, he foretold of a great white whale that would rise out of Witch Pond. Amos added to the legend by telling another story of the legendary giant, Moshup, who dug a secret tunnel from the cliffs to Witch Pond, so his pet white whale could seek safety and refuge. According to Manning, a tradition continues that when fog is seen over Witch Pond or felt in the air, Wampanoags say that the White Whale is spouting her plume.

Edwin DeVries Vanderhoop was born in 1848 in Gay Head to Surinamese-Dutch whaler, William Adrian Vanderhoop, and his Wampanoag wife, Beulah Oocouch Saulsbury. Edwin joined the Union army naval division at the age of 16, and was stationed on the USS Mahaska during the Civil War. After the war, he worked briefly on whalers before attending Wayland Seminary in Washington, D.C. He and his family eventually made their way back to Gay Head. In 1887, he became the county commissioner of Dukes County and the first Wampanoag to sit in the Legislature. He also managed a 19-room hotel he built called the Aquinnah House. The hotel was located on a hill overlooking the ocean, and years of strong winds and harsh weather pushed it into disrepair, giving it the appearance of a haunted house. Edwin's homestead, built in 1890, was listed on the National Register of Historic Places in 2006. It is currently operated as the Aquinnah Cultural Center and is the home of the Aquinnah Wampanoag Museum, featuring exhibits on Wampanoag tribal history and culture. The grounds and stone terrace of the center, which overlook the beautiful clay cliffs, are available for weddings and other events.

Deacon **Simon Johnson**, born in Gay Head in 1794, was a religious and political leader who also managed the Massachusetts Humane Society Gay Head Lifesaving Station. The station was established in 1895 and kept in service until the early 1950s; it was later replaced by Station Menemsha. He signed many petitions to the Commonwealth of Massachusetts, including one requesting Penal Laws to punish anyone who harvested cranberry bogs without the Wampanoag tribe's permission. It was rumored he only left the island three times in his life; two of which were journeys to Boston to deliver anti-liquor petitions to the General Court.

The second English explorer to land on Martha's Vineyard, which was called Capawack or Capawe, was **Captain Edward Harlow** in 1611. During his voyage, he took five Native Americans captive, including **Epenow**, and returned with them to London. Epenow, who was described as being great in stature, was put on display and taught to speak, "welcome, welcome" in English. This continued for three years; during this time, Epenow devised a plot to trick his captors into returning to Martha's Vineyard by telling them of a gold mine on the island. In June of 1614, they returned to Epenow's native island, and were peacefully greeted by the Wampanoags, including some of Epenow's brothers and cousins. The captain entertained the visitors to his ship, and invited them to return the next morning with trade goods. To prevent Epenow from escaping, he was accompanied at all times by three guards, and clothed in long garments that could be easily grabbed. Nevertheless, Epenow had secretly told his family that he was held captive, and the next morning they came with twenty canoes. Epenow called out in English for his friends to come aboard, but then dove overboard under cover of arrows being shot from the canoes. Both parties sustained heavy casualties, but Epenow survived the ordeal and by some accounts, went on to become a sachem.

Harrison Vanderhoop, also known as Chief No-Ho-No, nominated his nephew, **Donald F. Malonson**, to become his successor in 1951. Donald was born in Gay Head and attended the one room schoolhouse in town. He served in the 61st United States Naval Construction Battalion in the South Pacific during World War II and was honorably discharged on Oct. 10, 1945. Malonson, also known as Chief Running

Deer, symbolically led the Wampanoag Tribe of Gay Head from 1951 until his death in 2003. His son, F. Ryan Malonson, is the tribe's current chief.

Gladys A. Widdiss, née Gladys Malonson and sister of Chief Donald F. Malonson, was born in Gay Head in 1914. She graduated as valedictorian of her class from Tisbury High School in 1932. She moved to Boston for many years, where she married and worked various jobs. When her husband passed away, she sold their home and moved back to Gay Head. Serving as President of the Aquinnah Wampanoag of Gay Head from 1978 to 1987, Gladys was instrumental in the movement to gain federal recognition for the tribe. The Wampanoag acquired the Gay Head cliffs, the cranberry bogs surrounding Gay Head, and the Herring Creek during her tenure. In addition to being a historian and tribal elder, Gladys was also an artisan. One of the few people to receive an official permit from Gay Head to collect and use colored clay, her creations have been displayed all over the world. She passed away in 2012 at the age of 97 and is buried in the Aquinnah cemetery.

The Aquinnah Wampanoag are led by tribal council chair **Cheryl Andrews-Maltais**, who was elected to the post in November 2007 and re-elected as chairperson of the Wampanoag Tribe of Gay Head (Aquinnah) tribal council in November 2022. It is her fifth term as tribal chairperson. In 2020, for the first time in its history the vote was conducted by mail-in ballot because of the pandemic. Andrews-Maltais put forward plans for the development of an Aquinnah reservation casino, which was met with opposition by state and local officials. The tribe used a New Mexico-based third-party voting company to conduct the election. The company opened the ballots on Island Sunday with tribal chief **Ryan Malonson** and tribal medicine man **Jason Baird** present.

Do You Know – Aquinnah?

According to **Wampanoag legend**, the giant Moshup lived on Martha's Vineyard and caught whales off the coast. To kill the whale, he would fling it onto the cliffs then roast it over a fire that continually burned. The blood from the whales stained the cliffs the dark red that we see today.

The **Wampanoag Tribal logo** features an image of the larger than life Moshup holding up a whale in his left hand. The red cliffs of Aquinnah, where the giant had his den, stand majestically in the background.

In 2021, the National Park Service's **National Underground Railroad Network to Freedom Program** added the Martha's Vineyard African American Heritage Trail site "Randall Burton," and "Edgar Jones" on West Basin Road. The site honors the role the Wampanoag tribe played in the 1854 escape of Randall Burton, as well as another slave named Edgar Jones. Burton was a fugitive slave who escaped as a stowaway on the freight ship, *The Franklin,* out of Charlestown, South Carolina. The captain, upon discovering Burton, was adamant about returning the escaped slave. However, when the ship docked at Holmes Hole (present day Vineyard Haven), the fugitive stole a small boat and made his way to Gay Head. He was helped by several members of the Wampanoag tribe, and eventually made his way to abolitionists in New Bedford. His final fate is unknown. This was the second site on the island to join the program; the first site on the island was Edgartown Harbor.

Historian **John Warner Barber** described Aquinnah in 1841 as follows, "to those who are on board a vessel sailing near to shore, especially after a rain, and when the sun shines on it, it is a beautiful and brilliant object, hence the name Gay Head."

In 1965, **Gay Head Cliffs** were designated as a National Natural Landmark by the National Park Service.

Toad Rock Preserve, located at the intersection of State Road and Moshup Trail, is named for the large, glacially deposited rock on the northeastern portion of the property. According to Wampanoag legend, it was the pet toad of Moshup, the legendary giant, and turned into stone every time he left the island. The stone was also used as a type of "post office" for tribal members, who placed notes to each other on the rock when they passed by. The 6.3 acres preserve is maintained by the Martha's Vineyard Land Bank Commission and offers trails for hiking, biking, and horseback riding, as well as scenic views.

The **Gay Head Light**, which sits atop the cliffs, was the first lighthouse on Martha's Vineyard and was completed in 1799. After its completion, Paul Revere provided copper and tin to augment its weatherproofing. It was first moved back from the eroding cliffs in 1844. The original lighthouse was an octagonal wooden structure; in 1856, a new brick tower, which still stands today, was constructed to replace the older one. It is the only lighthouse on the east coast that flashes a beam pattern of three whites and one red. In 2015, the lighthouse was moved a second time, 134 feet from where it had originally been built.

Former First Lady Jacqueline Kennedy Onassis bought a 340-acre estate in 1979 called **Red Gate Farm**. Highlights of the family estate include views of Squibnocket Pond from almost every room of the main house, more than a mile of private beachfront, two freshwater ponds, a vegetable garden, and a blueberry patch. Caroline Kennedy Schlossberg, Jacqueline's daughter, inherited the property following her mother's death in 1994. In 2019, the family listed the property for sale with an initial asking price of $65 million. The following September, the Sheriff's Meadow Foundation and Martha's Vineyard Land Bank bought the 304 acre parcel of undeveloped land, while Caroline's family retained approximately 95 acres around their home site. The Land Bank acquired property is now known as the **Squibnocket Pond Reservation** and includes half a mile of Atlantic coast beachfront reached via trails; one mile of shoreline on Squibnocket Pond; two freshwater ponds, Lily Pond and Witch Pond; and loop trails, paddling access, and opportunities to swim, fish, and enjoy nature. Trails are now open to the public.

Canadian-American actor **Michael J. Fox** and his wife, Tracy Pollan, have four children including a set of identical daughters. One of his daughters is named Aquinnah after the town where his wife's family has a home.

Corinna Kaufman runs a seasonal art gallery from her home on Mariners View Lane. The **Seaweed Art Gallery** celebrates Victorian-era seaweed art, and Corinna's beautiful creations are available for sale at her workshop and gallery. Each piece of art is created using seaweed specifically chosen from the ocean by the artist.

For 15 years, the **Native American Artisan Market and Festival** has been held in July in Aquinnah. The fair offers traditional and contemporary artisan items; live music; interactive crafts, such as wampum drilling and sinew weaving; and local confections.

Cranberries have always been an important part of Wampanoag life, culminating in **Cranberry Day**, their most important holiday. In the past, it was a multi-day celebration of harvesting, feasting, and dancing. Cranberries were then shipped to New Bedford via catboat to exchange for staples such as sugar and molasses. The tradition of Cranberry Day continues today, on the second Tuesday of October each year. Families come together to harvest, with elders sharing stories and recollections of the past. At night, there is a community wide pot luck to celebrate and give thanks for another successful harvest.

Devil's Bridge is a shoal off the coast of Aquinnah near Gay Head Cliff that runs northwest towards the island of Cuttyhunk. According to Wampanoag legend, Moshup the giant missed living on the mainland, so he decided to build a bridge to it from Martha's Vineyard. As he was gathering huge boulders in the sound, a crab bit his toe. He dropped all the boulders, forming Devil's Bridge.

On January 18, 1884, the passenger steamer *City of Columbus* was wrecked on Devil's Bridge. Of the 45 officers and 87 passengers, only 17 crew and 12 passengers survived, making this shipwreck one of the worst ocean disasters of all time.

Thursday is Pizza Night at the **Orange Peel Bakery**. From April to November, stop by for a 12-inch pizza between 5 and 8 pm for eat-in or take-out. Prices start at $15 and go up based on toppings; they also offer a gluten-free cauliflower crust. Make sure to Bring Your Own Beer, and hang around for owner and baker Juli Vanderhoop's crispy deliciousness baked in her wood-fired oven.

There is a scene in the timeless classic, *Jaws*, where Martin Brody and Matt Hooper, played by Roy Scheider and Richard Dreyfuss, have an argument with Mayor Vaughn (played by Murray Hamilton) because he doesn't want to close the beaches. Gay Head Light can be seen in the background.

Aquinnah Town Center was classified as a historic district by the National Register of Historic Places in 1999. It includes six buildings and two monuments based around the intersection of South and Church Streets: an 1844 schoolhouse that serves as the town's library; the 1850 Gay Head Community Baptist Church; the 1856 minister's parsonage house; the 1929 town hall; a former post office from the 1920s; a small, unused outhouse on the church property; and two monuments commemorating the town's contributions to World War I.

Sassafras is an indigenous Wôpanâak nonprofit on Nôepe (Martha's Vineyard) founded in 2003. Its mission is to offer programs, events and trainings that reconnect youth and adults to the earth through indigenous mentoring, to create a truly equitable community space, and to restore earth-centered regenerative indigenous cultures.

Sassafras preserves traditional knowledge, cultivates wisdom, and restores balance using earth-centered education. Youth exposed to this model become rooted individuals that are deeply connected to "our mother the earth." They develop character and regenerative leadership qualities, and become deeply invested in giving back to their communities and the earth.

Question: What does this picture depict?

Answer on page 23

All About Chilmark

Chilmark, located on the western edge of Martha's Vineyard, includes the quaint fishing village of Menemsha. With a population of approximately 1,200 (as of the 2020 United States Census), it is primarily a residential area, with some of the highest property values not only on the island, but in Massachusetts as well. It has the second smallest population, but is growing steadily, with a 40% increase in residents between 2010 and 2020. Geographically, it encompasses 19 square miles and includes the island of Noman's Land, which lies three miles southwest of Martha's Vineyard. It is bordered by Vineyard Sound to the north, Aquinnah to the west, West Tisbury to the east, and the Atlantic Ocean to the south. It is the least densely populated town on Martha's Vineyard.

The town draws its name from the ancestral home of **Governor Thomas Mayhew of Tisbury**, in the English county of Wiltshire. Thomas Mayhew and his son, Thomas, were Watertown merchants who acquired Martha's Vineyard, Nantucket, and the Elizabeth islands as a proprietary colony from William Alexander, the Second Earl of Sterling, and Sir Ferdinando Gorges in 1641. William Alexander did not hold undisputed title to the land. Although he received a royal grant of coastal lands in 1635, the explorer Sir Fernando Gorges also had a claim. This is why Thomas Mayhew needed to receive confirmation from both men to settle the islands.

Chilmark incorporated on September 14, 1694 and was the first town on Martha's Vineyard to separate from the two original towns of Tisbury and Edgartown. In 1714, Chilmark became a township, including the island of Noman's Land. This aptly named island is uninhabited

Answer from page 22: Moving the Gay Head Lighthouse

and encompasses 612 acres. In fact, the island's name most likely came from the Martha's Vineyard Wampanoag sachem, Tequenoman, who had jurisdiction over the island when the English first began exploring the area in the early 1600s. This small island has an interesting history. The United States Navy built an airfield on the island and used Nomans Land Range, an aerial gunnery, from 1943 to 1996. In 1998, the Navy transferred ownership to the United States Fish and Wildlife Service. The Service had managed the eastern area of the island since 1975, and now devoted the entire area for use as an unstaffed wildlife refuge, particularly for migratory birds. Nomans Land Island National Wildlife Refuge, which is approximately 30% wetlands, provides important habitat to many guilds of birds including: double-crested cormorants, Virginia rails, Savannah sparrows, Leach's storm-petrels, and numerous species of raptors (such as peregrine falcons and Cooper's hawks). Due to safety risks from unexploded ordnance and its value as a wildlife habitat, the island is closed to all public use.

Menemsha, which is a quaint fishing village within the town of Chilmark, is located on the northeast coast on Menemsha Pond where it empties into Vineyard Sound. While most of Chilmark is residential, Menemsha does have a small working harbor. In addition, there are charter boats to the nearby Elizabeth Islands, a United States Coast Guard station, and Menemsha Hills Reservation. Owned by the Trustees of Reservation, Menemsha Hills offers 211 acres of low wetlands, woodland groves, coastal plains, and 308-foot Prospect Hill. The Brickyard Trail, a moderately challenging 3.2 mile round trip hike, leads to the Menemsha Hills Reservation Beach, which is very rocky. There are seldom swimmers at this beach.

Menemsha Public Beach has gentle surf, making it perfect for families with young children. Take in the scenic views of Cuttyhunk and the other Elizabeth islands, hunt for crabs in the surf, or enjoy a photo worthy sunset on the beach. Parking is limited, so plan to arrive early. Lifeguards are on duty during the summer season, and public restrooms are a short walk from the beach. A small store nearby sells ice, drinks and snack items as well as gasoline.

Squibnocket Beach, or "Squibby" as it's called by the locals, is a residents-only beach along the south side of Chilmark on the Atlantic Ocean. With a rocky coast and strong surf, it's a popular beach for surfing. A 44-space parking area was added as part of a beach project in 2018 and offers a short walk to the waves. There are no lifeguards on duty and dogs, nude sunbathing, and cliff climbing are prohibited. Stonewall Beach, to the east of Squibnocket, is a private beach that draws few crowds.

Another town beach for residents is **Lucy Vincent Beach**. The woman after whom the beach was named was a Chilmark librarian and the first woman in town to own an automobile. Ever bucking convention and gender norms, Lucy fought back when the town told her shellfish permits were not issued to women, becoming the first of her gender to obtain one. One of Lucy's wishes upon her death was to donate a portion of her 60-acre property for use as a town beach. As this beach is also on the Atlantic, expect strong surf. There are also stunning views of the cliffs and other rock formations.

Source: "What Did Lucy Think?" by Peter Simon in 8/1/17 edition of Martha's Vineyard Magazine.

If you don't mind a short hike and enjoy getting off the beaten path, be sure to visit **Great Rock Bight Beach**. Managed by the Martha's Vineyard Land Bank Commission, this property features wide, graceful trails that wind through open meadows and woodlands to a sandy beach. Located east of Menemsha Hills and The Brickyard, the preserve is reached via Brickyard Road, a narrow, dirt lane that runs about a half-mile to the parking area. The beach features a large boulder just beyond the surf that gives the place its name, and it offers a quarter-mile stretch of sand that is just perfect for a sunny afternoon of sunbathing. There is no lifeguard on duty here. This also may be the best spot anywhere on the island to watch the sunset. It is also the first stop on the Martha's Vineyard African American Heritage Trail.

There are a series of small ponds along the Atlantic including **Chilmark Pond, Quenames Cove**, and **Black Point Pond**. The town shares **Tisbury Great Pond** to the east and **Menemsha Pond** and **Squibnocket Pond** to the southwest, along the Aquinnah town line. It is between these two latter ponds that the only road to Aquinnah passes. Long Beach, privately owned, runs along the southern side of Squibnocket Pond and technically connects the towns. At one point in the late 17th and early 18th century, Squibnocket Pond was open to the sea. However, the barrier beach with its sand dunes eventually closed this opening permanently. Occasionally in winter storms, waves wash across low points in the beach, but the beach itself has not been breached in a hundred years, unlike other barrier beaches on Martha's Vineyard.

People of Significance – Chilmark

A modest paragraph in the Vineyard Gazette of December 15, 1882 announced the opening of a lending library in the Quitsa section of Chilmark with thirty-three books donated by **Alice Stone Blackwell** and her cousin **Florence Blackwell Mayhew** (Mrs. E. Eliot Mayhew). The charge for book rentals was fixed at 3 cents a week. The books were kept on a shelf in the **Mayhew Brothers'** (later E. Eliot Mayhew's) store across the road from the Mayhew homestead. Expenses of the first library were $32.04 for the building of a bookcase. This appears to have been the first public library on Martha's Vineyard.

In the town report for 1915, **Grove Ryan's** name first appeared as having done painting for the library, work which he continued faithfully for more than forty-eight years.

The story of a community store in Chilmark began in the early 1900's and was known as **E. Eliot Mayhew's** store before the site of the current **Chilmark Store**. There is a sign that proclaims, "The people of Chilmark used to gather at a store owned and operated by E. Elliot

Mayhew who had a sign on his building which proclaimed that he was the dealer of almost anything."

Do You Know – Chilmark?

The **Grey Barn and Farm** is the Island's only organic farm and produces nationally recognized cheeses; milk and eggs; artisanal, fresh baked breads; and veggies, poultry, and meats, all set amid the rolling grounds of Chilmark, with an architecturally distinct, modern-minimalist design of the farm compound.

Chilmark Public Library is a full-service free library on Martha's Vineyard, with a collection of 34,000 items and over 50,000 digital titles. The library was established in 1882 and was the first public library on Martha's Vineyard.

The **Brickyard** was a water-powered brickworks operation on the north shore of Chilmark. It was established in 1642 and was the first of its kind in New England and passed through multiple owners until it was decommissioned in the late 19th century.

When residents say they are going **"Up-Island,"** they mean they are heading to the western areas of Aquinnah, Chilmark, Menemsha, and West Tisbury. The designation is based on nautical terminology, where heading west means going "up" in longitude. Menemsha was the shooting background for the fictional "Amity Island" of Steven Spielberg's 1975 film *Jaws*.

Martha's Vineyard Sign Language (MVSL) was a village sign-language that was once widely used on the island of Martha's Vineyard from the early 18th century to 1952. It was used by both Deaf and hearing people in the community; consequently, deafness did not become a barrier to participation in public life. Deaf people who signed Martha's Vineyard Sign Language were extremely independent. They participated in society as typical citizens, although there were incidents of discrimination, and language barriers.

The language was able to thrive because of the unusually high percentage of Deaf islanders and because deafness was a recessive trait, which meant that almost anyone might have both Deaf and hearing siblings. In 1854, when the island's Deaf population peaked, an average of one person in 155 was Deaf, while the United States national average was one in about 5,730. In the town of Chilmark, which had the highest concentration of Deaf people on the island, the average was 1 in 25; at one point, in a section of Chilmark called Squibnocket, as much as 1 in 4 of the population of 60 was Deaf.

Sign language on the island declined when the population migrated to the mainland. There are no fluent signers of MVSL today. Katie West, the last Deaf person born into the island's sign-language tradition, died in 1952, though there were a few elderly residents still able to recall MVSL when researchers started examining the language in the 1980s. Linguists are working to save the language, but their task is difficult because they cannot experience MVSL firsthand.

Chilmark has the highest point on Martha's Vineyard, at the 311-foot summit of Peaked Hill.

Noman's Land, the island off the southwestern shore of Chilmark was once a small fishing village like Menemsha. It was evacuated during World War II when it was used by the Navy as a practice bombing range,

There was a time when a person could stand anywhere in Chilmark and **see the ocean**.

On March 5, 1982, **John Belushi** died and was buried four days later in Abel's Hill Cemetery in Chilmark. Belushi often visited the Vineyard and his family felt it fitting to bury him there. The epitaph on his gravestone reads: "Though I may be gone, Rock and Roll lives on." Because of the many visitors to his grave and the threat of vandalism, his body was moved somewhere near the grave site. His grave remains a popular site for visitors to Chilmark and they often leave tokens in memory of the late comedian.

In August 2009, 2010 and 2011, **President Barack Obama** and his family vacationed in Chilmark, renting the **Blue Heron Farm**.

The **Coast Guard Station** burned to the ground in July 2010 but was rebuilt and recommissioned in April 2015.

On the television show *The X-Files*, Fox Mulder was raised in Chilmark. His younger sister Samantha's alien abduction happened in Chilmark on November 27, 1973.

At the Hirshhorn Museum in Washington, D.C., there is a 1920 painting by artist **Thomas Hart Benton** called *People of Chilmark*. Benton first visited Chilmark in the summer of 1919. *People of Chilmark* was the artist's first masterpiece and, at 5½' × 6½', the largest painting he had executed to date.

The **Menemsha Bike Ferry**, is a twenty-five-foot pontoon boat with bench seats down the sides, driven by an electric outboard and two ranks of batteries stowed beneath the seats. It can carry pedestrians, strollers, dogs, and of course, bikes – up to six at a time. It travels from Menemsha to a boat launch on the Aquinnah side of the channel. It runs 9 am to 5 pm. It closes during the winter months.

Thomas Hart Benton, of Kansas City, MO, is one of America's most famous fine artists. **Denys Wortman** is a cartoonist, the creator of *Mopey Dick and the Duke*, a widely syndicated newspaper cartoon. Benton and Wortman have been meeting at Martha's Vineyard near a place called **Beetlebung Corners** in Chilmark for the past 30 summers.

Tom Fenton issues a challenge of artistic talents in a match to see which artist could produce the better portrait of the other. The results appeared in Collier's magazine. One art critic, opined, "The two paintings demonstrate impressive facility in technique, tremendous power, and extraordinary balance of subject matter with philosophical intent."

The **Allen Farm in Chilmark** is the oldest continuously working family farm on the Island, now being lovingly stewarded by its 12th generation of caretakers. Among the 100 waterfront acres, you'll find rustic stone walls, a 200-year-old farmhouse and outbuildings, and some very photogenic horses, miniature donkeys, and sheep. The land on the ocean has been preserved so that the view of the ocean will always be available from the meadow.

One of the most fascinating stories of Chilmark involves the old **Chilmark Cemetery** located on **North Road**. While it is not known who specifically built the cemetery or when, local legend speaks of a Native American tribe that was rumored to inhabit the area hundreds of years ago.

The cemetery also contains a few mysterious gravestones with inscriptions that remain unsolved to this day. Some believe these gravestones belong to unknown victims of an old war between two rival tribes, while others think they are from more recent times and are just forgotten graves with unmarked occupants.

In addition to its mysterious cemetery, Chilmark is known for other eerie tales as well. Tales abound about haunting spirits that wander around town late at night, making their presence known through strange sounds and smells. Some locals have even reported seeing apparitions near their homes or hearing strange noises coming from deep in the woods surrounding the town.

Finally, some believe that Chilmark holds many secrets beneath its surface - literally! There are rumors that an ancient temple lies beneath one of the many lakes in the area, filled with treasure and long-forgotten artifacts waiting to be discovered. Whether these stories have any truth or not remains a mystery, but those brave enough to venture out looking for answers may find themselves lucky enough to stumble upon something extraordinary!

All About Edgartown

Edgartown is a tourist destination on the island of Martha's Vineyard in Dukes County, for which it is the county seat. It was once a major whaling port, with historic houses that have been carefully preserved. Today it hosts yachting events around its large harbor. It includes the smaller island of Chappaquiddick.

Edgartown is a part of Massachusetts's 9th congressional district, represented in the Massachusetts Senate as a portion of the Cape and Islands district. The town's population was 5,168 at the 2020 census.

In 1642, **Rev. Thomas Mayhew, Jr**. led a group of families to start a colony on the island after its purchase by his father Thomas Mayhew. Originally called Great Harbor, it was incorporated on July 8, 1671, as Edgar Towne, named for Edgar, whose father James II of England, was heir presumptive to the English throne. Those who chose the name to honor the monarchy did not know Edgar had died at the age of three on June 8, 1671. It was one of the two original towns on Martha's Vineyard, along with Tisbury, incorporated at the same time.

The younger Mayhew became the first church planting Protestant missionary after he settled in Edgartown. A Wampanoag Indian named Hiacoomes who lived nearby became his partner in founding the churches in the Indian communities.

Edgartown was one of the primary ports for the whaling industry during the 1800s. Ships from all over the world would dock in its sheltered bay and captains would build grand mansions for their families with ornate top floor rooms called widow's walks, which overlooked the harbor. A myth developed that wives would watch for months from these tiny rooms, hoping to see the sails of ships that would bring their husbands home from the sea. There is little or no evidence that widow's walks were intended or regularly used for this purpose. They were frequently built around the chimney of the residence, thus creating an easy access route to the structure, allowing the residents of the home to pour sand down burning chimneys in the event of a chimney fire in the hopes of preventing the house from burning down.

As more economical alternatives became available the whaling industry began to decline. By the beginning of the 20th century, its influence on the tiny town which had made its fortunes through the industry, ended. Today the town is more known for tourism.

Edgartown was an old whaling port and is now a summer and tourist destination with a multitude of houses built by whaling captains and other prominent people of prior centuries. The growth of the population over the past 25 years has led to a period of intense renewal of these old houses. Water Street along the harbor is the location of many of these "Captain's Homes" which line both sides of the street. The town has also encouraged renovation of historical structures. As part of this effort, the Whaling Church, a large 18th-century church, has been converted to a performing arts center and the adjacent Daniel Fisher House is now used for a variety of social functions. In addition to the architectural draw of the town, Edgartown is easily traversed on foot or bicycle, making it attractive to tourists.

The **Edgartown Harbor Light** at the end of north Water Street defines the entrance to the Harbor. The harbor is large and entered through a modest sized channel on the North side of Edgartown. It opens into **Katama Bay**, created by a barrier beach that sometimes connects the south end of Chappaquiddick to the remainder of Edgartown, the barrier beach opened during a spring storm in 2007. This has led to a 3-knot current through Katama Bay and **Edgartown Harbor**. This protected body of water provides ample mooring for small and large boats. The opening of the harbor will accommodate large sailing and motorized boats but will not accommodate large ships or yachts, which may anchor outside the harbor.

Another feature is **South Beach**, a small part of the ocean beach that runs the entire southern length of the island from Edgartown to Aquinnah. It can be reached by driving or riding the bus south from Edgartown center for approximately 2.5 miles. South Beach is a crashing ocean beach. It is a major destination for tourists. Much of the beach in

Edgartown is open to the public with ample parking available. The section of the beach near Katama is often crowded, while the sections further to the west (near Edgartown Great Pond and Oyster Pond) are often less so.

People of Significance - Edgartown

Ruth Gordon Jones (October 30, 1896 – August 28, 1985) was an American actress, screenwriter, and playwright. She began her career performing on Broadway at age 19. Known for her nasal voice and distinctive personality, Gordon gained international recognition and critical acclaim for film roles that continued into her 70s and 80s. Her later work included performances in *Rosemary's Baby* (1968), *What Ever Happened to Aunt Alice?* (1969), *Where's Poppa?* (1970), *Harold and Maude* (1971), *Every Which Way But Loose* (1978), and *Any Which Way You Can* (1980).

On August 28, 1985, Gordon died at her summer home in Edgartown, Massachusetts, following a stroke at age 88. Her husband for 43 years, **Garson Kanin**, was at her side and said that even her last day of life was typically full, with walks, talks, errands, and a morning of work on a new play. She had made her last public appearance two weeks before, at a benefit showing of the film *Harold and Maude* and had recently finished acting in four films.

Patricia Neal died at her home in Edgartown, Martha's Vineyard, Massachusetts, on August 8, 2010, from lung cancer. She was 84 years old. She had become a Catholic four months before she died and was buried in the Abbey of Regina Laudis in Bethlehem, Connecticut, where the actress Dolores Hart, her friend since the early 1960s, had become a nun and ultimately prioress. Neal had been a longtime supporter of the abbey's open-air theatre and arts program.

E. Michael Quinlan, Naval Academy graduate, Navy pilot, lawyer, and publisher has two homes in Edgartown where his wife, Jeanne and five daughters have long enjoyed their summers in Edgartown. Now there are husbands and grandchildren to share their enjoyment. Mike shared many sailings with another Edgartown resident, Walter Cronkite.

Walter Cronkite, America's most famous television newsman, was a summer resident of Edgartown between 1974 and 2009. He owned a waterfront 1.3 acre property in Edgartown and kept his 43-foot, ketch-rigged yacht, Wyntje, which was moored at the dock at 40 Green Hollow for many years. He is well remembered for lending his time to many fundraisers on the Island.

South Water Street is dominated by a huge pagoda tree brought from China as a seedling by **Captain Thomas Milton** in the early days of the last century. It was brought to Edgartown to grace his new home then being built in Edgartown, and has been growing on the island ever since.

Captain Valentine Pease's home, a Greek Revival house, has a lot of history, tied to literature and the whaling industry that shaped Edgartown in the 19th century. The home was built around 1830 for Captain Valentine Pease (1797-1870), a master mariner and captain of the *Acushnet*, a prominent whaling vessel which often departed from New Bedford. In 1841, Captain Valentine Pease, his crew, and a 21-year-old Herman Melville shipped out of New Bedford for eighteen months as Melville's only whaling voyage. Melville took part in the hunting and killing of whales and in harvesting and processing whale oil aboard ship. He endured gales and calm, experienced excitement and boredom, followed ship's discipline, all the while absorbing the lore of the veteran seamen who made up the *Acushnet's* diverse and colorful crew. It is speculated that Valentine Pease was an inspiration for the character of Captain Ahab in Melville's book, "Moby Dick."

Thomas Henry Chirgwin, an Edgartown native in search of a new endeavor after selling his Oak Bluffs plumbing business, built the Colonial Inn which opened as a hotel in 1911. The business endeavor began modestly with a somewhat small house of 16 rooms on the site of the current Vineyard Square Hotel & Suites. It was conceived of as an upscale, in town resort. When it opened that year, the Colonial Inn was described as finished in Old English style, and furnished with every modern convenience. "The rooms are large and airy, with many superb water views, and the beds are famous for their comfort. Three dining rooms serve the pleasure of guests, and the table in variety and cuisine will continue to be unsurpassed." The Inn's ads also heralded being electrically lighted, having Wintucket Spring Water, hot and cold baths, and all rooms being steam heated for winter patronage. All of this was "finely located" just one minute from Steamboat Wharf.

Mark Hess is the manager of the Edgartown Golf Club, a job he has held for 34 years. Mr. Hess recently added author to his impressive golf resume with *You Don't Have a Prayer*, a tribute to his place of employment.

The **Edgartown Golf Club** was created in 1926 by Cornelius Lee, who, like Mr. Hess, had a vision and largely completed it by himself. Enamored of the Old Course at St. Andrews, Mr. Lee decided to create a similar course on his Edgartown property, Mr. Hess writes in the first chapter of his book, which takes the reader deep into the club history:

"No architect was used and the only help he had was Bror Hogland, who was the first greenskeeper," Mr. Hess writes. "Mr. Hogland has said that the only help that he had was from Cyrus Norton, who led a horse that was supplied by Orin Morton, to plough the fairways, tees and greens."

Do You Know – Edgartown?

There is a Japanese style garden on Chappaquiddick Island. There are several walking paths which lead past a pond, arched footbridge, and rock gardens. It is named **"M-Y-T-O-I."**

The original **Edgartown Light** was a wooden, Cape Cod-style, two-story Keeper's house built on wood piles a short distance offshore in shallow water. For the first two years of service, this offshore location required the Keeper to row a short distance.

There are nine beaches, a yacht club, and several preserves and reservations in the town of Edgartown, including the **Wasque Reservation** along the south shore of **Chappaquiddick** and the **Cape Pogue Wildlife Refuge** along the east shore of the island.

There are two lighthouses in the town, the **Cape Pogue Light** on Chappaquiddick and the **Edgartown Harbor Light** in Edgartown Harbor.

Old Whaling Church is a landmark built in 1843. Originally built for Methodist whaling captains and other seafarers, the place of worship was designed by **Frederick Baylies, Jr.** in the Greek Revival style with a Gothic Revival clock tower. Inside, visitors will notice the curved ceiling, massive timbers, and original whale oil lamps in the main hall.

The Christina, a schooner out at sea on her way to Boston from New York, was carrying cement and five crew members when she was obliterated by gale-force winds and capsized off the coast of Chappaquiddick Island. Four of the men perished by the time help could reach the vessel four days later, and the lone survivor miraculously clung to the ship's mast for 56 hours, after which both of his feet and his fingers required amputation. More than 150 years later, an assemblage of wooden planks and rusty iron bolts were found poking out of East Beach on Chappaquiddick Island.

Auto transportation to Chappaquiddick is provided by two ferries, the "On Time II" and "On Time III". A common myth is that the original ferry "On Time" was given its name because the ferry has never had scheduled runs and thus is never late. In fact, the ferry was given this name because a new owner, **Foster B. Silva** of Chappaquiddick, had less than two weeks to build it before taking over the service on August 1, 1948. The work crew—led by **Captain Samuel B. Norton** and master boatbuilder **Manuel Swartz Roberts**, both of Edgartown—built and launched the new ferry "on time."

The best place to enjoy the spectacular ocean view, including the Edgartown Lighthouse and Chappaquiddick Island, is from one of the rocking chairs that line the **Harbor View Hotel's porch**.

One of the classic iconic landmarks is **The Carnegie**, a neoclassic structured library building offering access to the public. Inside, you will find the renovated and restored landmark including reading rooms, a visitor center, gift shop and the permanent exhibition, **Living Landmarks**, which illustrates the historical development of Martha's Vineyard through the lens of the landmarks in Vineyard Trust's care.

Felix Neck is about three miles outside the center of town on Vineyard Haven Road. The two hundred acres, owned by the **Massachusetts Audubon Society**, provide marked trails and a program of wildlife management and conservation education throughout the year. It is located at One Hundred Felix Neck Drive in Edgartown.

The library at the Martha's Vineyard Museum in Edgartown has an extensive collection of materials about the Island's deaf population, including notes from **Alexander Graham Bell** (the inventor of the telephone was also a teacher of the deaf, who came to the Vineyard to study the occurrences late in the nineteenth century).

Katama was the terminus of the Martha's Vineyard Railroad. The train **Active** ran between the **Oak Bluffs Wharf** and **Mattakeeset Lodge** in Katama. The Mattakeeset Lodge (note the spelling variations of Mattakesett) was located on the shore of Katama Bay. A portion of the Mattakeeset lodge, including one tower, was incorporated into a wing of the Harbor View Hotel in Edgartown.

South Beach runs the entire length of the southern end of Martha's Vineyard; however, the name "South Beach" commonly refers to a stretch of public beach that is demarcated by Herring Creek Road on the west and Chappaquiddick Island on the east.

The word "Katama" comes from a Wampanoag word meaning "crab-fishing place." It is sometimes referred to as the "Great Plains."

Katama Airfield is unique. It has three airstrips, more than most small airports, and sightlines of South Beach and the Atlantic Ocean.

Princess Diana chose to stay at **The Charlotte's Inn** in Edgartown while on Martha's Vineyard. The owner of the inn, Gery Conover, and his son, Tim, were able to make her stay as paparazzi-free as possible, and she was so grateful for the peaceful vacation, she threw a thank-you party for the duo.

Edgartown was used as the main shooting location for the town of Amity in Steven Spielberg's 1975 blockbuster Jaws. Many landmarks and buildings in Edgartown that were filmed in the movie can still be seen today.

Edgartown is located at the eastern end of Martha's Vineyard referred to as "down-island", a vestige of the island's traditional maritime manner of speaking in that as a ship travels east, it is said to be traveling "down east" as longitude decreases towards the Prime Meridian.

The town of Edgartown includes the smaller island of **Chappaquiddick**, sometimes connected to the rest of Martha's Vineyard by a barrier beach which can be breached during storms.

Edgartown is close to **Nantucket's Muskeget Island**, which is seven miles east of **Wasque Point**, the southeasternmost point of Chappaquiddick.

Edgartown is among the most northerly locations with a semitropical climate in North America. In 1874, **Old Colony Railroad** founded the Martha's **Vineyard Railroad**. At one point, there was a railroad that ran on nine miles of track between what is now the Oak Bluffs Ferry Terminal to the long-gone Mattakeeset Lodge in Katama, Edgartown.

The first settlers named it **"Great Harbor".** Upon the town's incorporation on July 8, 1671, they changed the name to "Edgar Towne" after Prince Edgar, the young son of the current monarch, King James II. He died at the age of three.

Pink and green weekend was established in 2014. The weekend is a celebration of spring (and Mother's Day) and the entire town joins in the fun.

The **Edgartown Round the Island Race** is sponsored by the Edgartown Yacht Club. The very first race was held during the summer of 1939 and has been an annual tradition since then excluding the years of World War II.

Edgartown was once the nation's largest **whaling port** in the mid-1830's until it was succeeded by New Bedford.

In 1964, the Edgartown annual **town budget** was $400,000. Last year it was upwards of $30 million.

There is a legend that there is a blue rock somewhere on Chappaquiddick Island that marks the location of a pirate treasure. The story goes that one night in 1824, **James Roland Cooke**, a farmer from the area, overheard men discussing the location of a buried chest. Upon finding a spot near an odd blue rock that was a freshly dug and refilled hole, Cooke left to find a constable. Upon returning to the blue rock, however, the winds had smoothed over the exact location of the hole and Cooke was never able to locate the possible hoard again.

After major renovations that included a staircase to the **lantern room**, the interior of the Nantucket Lighthouse is open to the public.

Cannonball Park, sometimes referred to as Memorial Park, was dedicated on July 4, 1901, to seventy island soldiers who died in the Civil War and features multiple cannon and cannonball statues, benches and an obelisk.

You can climb to the top of the **Edgartown Lighthouse** where you will be rewarded with wonderful views.

The **Martha's Vineyard Airport** is a public airport located in the middle of the island of Martha's Vineyard, three miles south of the central business district of Vineyard Haven, in Dukes County. This airport is owned by Dukes County and lies on the border between the towns of West Tisbury and Edgartown. It is the largest of three airports and the only one on the island served by airlines. In addition to service from six commercial airlines, it is used by a significant number of general aviation aircraft. The other airports on the Island are Katama Airpark and Trade Wind Airport.

The airport identifier **MVY** has entered into general use as an abbreviation for the island of Martha's Vineyard and is often used for non-aviation purposes.

Question: Can you identify this lighthouse?

Answer on page 41

All About Oak Bluffs

Oak Bluffs, one of the island's principal points of arrival for summer tourists, is noted for its "gingerbread cottages" and other well-preserved mid- to late-nineteenth-century buildings. The town has been a historically important center of African American culture since the eighteenth century. The population was 5,341 at the 2020 United States Census.

The first inhabitants of Oak Bluffs were the **Wampanoag people**, who have lived on Martha's Vineyard (Wampanoag name: Noepe) for approximately 10,000 years. The area that is now Oak Bluffs was called **"Ogkeshkuppe,"** which means "damp/wet thicket or woods."

The area was later settled by Europeans in 1642 and was part of Edgartown until 1880, when it was officially incorporated as Cottage City. The town re-incorporated in 1907 as Oak Bluffs, named because the town was the site of an oak grove along the bluffs overlooking Nantucket Sound. Oak Bluffs was the only one of the six towns on the island to be consciously planned, and the only one developed specifically with tourism in mind.

People of **African descent** first arrived at Martha's Vineyard in the 1600s as enslaved West Africans who worked on the farms of European settlers. The Oak Bluffs harbor drew freed slaves, laborers and sailors in the 18th century, and white locals sold them land. After slavery was abolished, the freed blacks came to work in the fishing industries, in turn drawing black residents from the Massachusetts mainland, who came and started businesses to serve the Vineyard's growing population. During the 1800s, some Black laborers also worked as servants to wealthy white families and in the hotels.

Answer from page 40: Edgartown Lighthouse

In the late 19th and 20th centuries, middle-class blacks bought or rented summer homes, and many of their descendants returned annually. Formerly enslaved people, or their descendants, bought property around Baptist Temple Park in the early 20th century, drawn by the religious services held there. Teachers, politicians, lawyers, doctors, artists, musicians, and entrepreneurs resided there for decades afterward. Affluent African Americans from New York, Boston, and Washington came to Oak Bluffs, the only Martha's Vineyard town that welcomed Black tourists as other towns on the island did not allow Black guests to stay in inns and hotels until the 1960s. Many bought houses in an area they called the Oval or the Highlands, which Harlem Renaissance writer Dorothy West wrote about in her 1995 novel, *The Wedding* (edited by Doubleday editor Jacqueline Kennedy Onassis, a Vineyard resident who visited West for two summers).

By the 1930s, local Black landowners were transforming the town into the country's best-known and most exclusive African American vacation spot. Down the road from West, Adam Clayton Powell Jr. owned a cottage in the Oval where Arctic explorer Matthew Henson was a guest. Further down the road is Shearer Cottage, the first inn for African Americans vacationers. It was built by a Charles Shearer, the son of a slave, when Shearer saw that black visitors were not able to stay at the homes due to segregation. Guests at the inn included the first self-made American millionairess **Madame CJ Walker**, singers **Paul Robeson, Ethel Waters** and **Lillian Evanti**; and composer **Harry T. Burleigh**.

In 1866, **Robert Morris Copeland** was hired by a group of New England developers to design a planned residential community in Martha's Vineyard. The site, a large, rolling, treeless pasture overlooking Nantucket Sound, was adjacent to the immensely popular Methodist camp meeting, **Wesleyan Grove**, a curving network of narrow streets lined with quaint "Carpenter's Gothic" cottages, picket fences, and pocket parks. Seeking to take advantage of the camp's seasonal popularity (and overflowing population), the developers **established Oak Bluffs Land and Wharf Company**, gaining immediate success: Five hundred lots were sold between 1868 and 1871. Copeland would end up creating three plans for the community to accommodate its constant expansion.

Oak Bluffs is one of the earliest planned residential communities and largely informed later suburban development in the United States.

Some of the earliest visitors to the area that became **Cottage City** and later Oak Bluffs were Methodists, who gathered in the oak grove known as Wesleyan Grove each summer for multi-day religious "camp meetings" held under large tents and in the open air.

As families returned to the grove year after year, tents pitched on the ground gave way to tents pitched on wooden platforms and eventually to small wooden cottages. Small in scale and closely packed, the cottages grew more elaborate over time. Porches, balconies, elaborate door, and window frames became common, as did complex wooden scrollwork affixed to the roof edges as decorative trim. The unique "gingerbread" or "Carpenter's Gothic" architectural style of the cottages was often accented by the owner's use of bright, multi-hued paint schemes, which gave the summer cottages a quaint, almost storybook look.

Dubbed **"gingerbread cottages,"** they became a tourist attraction in their own right in the late nineteenth century. So, too, did the Tabernacle: a circular, open-sided pavilion covered by a metal roof supported by tall wrought iron columns, erected in the late 1880s, which became a venue for services and community events. The campground's gingerbread cottages are cherished historic landmarks as well as expensive real estate. Many are still family owned and passed on generation to generation. The cottages and the Tabernacle were added to the National Register of Historic Places in 1978, recognized in 2000 by the National Trust for Historic Preservation and declared a National Historic Landmark by the US Department of the Interior in 2005.

Nineteenth-century tourists, arriving by steamer from the mainland, could also choose from a wide range of secular attractions: shops, restaurants, ice cream parlors, dance halls, band concerts, walks along seaside promenades, or swims in the waters of Nantucket Sound. Resort hotels, of which the Wesley House is the sole surviving example, lined the waterfront and the bluffs. For a time, a narrow-gauge railway carried curious travelers from the steamship wharf in Oak Bluffs to Edgartown, running along tracks laid on what is now Joseph Sylvia State Beach. In 1884, the **Flying Horses Carousel** was brought to Oak Bluffs from

Coney Island and installed a few blocks inland from the ocean, where it remains in operation today. Built in 1876, it is the oldest platform carousel still in operation. Like the grounds and buildings of the Campground (so designated in April 2005), the Flying Horses were designated a National Historic Landmark by the Secretary of the Interior.

People of Significance – Oak Bluffs

Edward W. Brooke III, of Newton, MA, and Oak Bluffs, was the first African American politician to be popularly elected to the US Senate since the Reconstruction era, when he was elected as a Republican for Massachusetts. Before being elected into the senate, he was attorney general of Massachusetts. Although many in his party did not like that he was to enter the senate, he followed the advice of his mother: "keep fighting, if you work hard there is nothing you cannot do."

Upon being elected a U.S. Senator he was asked about where he would live and he responded by saying, "And, of course, we will never give up Martha's Vineyard. We love it there."

Henry Louis "Skip" Gates Jr. (born September 16, 1950) is an American literary critic, professor, historian, and filmmaker, who serves as the Alphonse Fletcher University Professor and Director of the Hutchins Center for African and African American Research at Harvard University. He is a Trustee of the Gilder Lehrman Institute of American History. He rediscovered the earliest African-American novels, long forgotten, and has published extensively on appreciating African-American literature as part of the Western canon. He has been summering on Martha's Vineyard since 1981 and currently owns the big white house in Harthaven.

Dorothy West was born in Boston, Massachusetts, on June 2, 1907, the only child of Virginian Isaac Christopher West, who was enslaved at birth and became a successful businessman, and Rachel Pease Benson of Camden, South Carolina, one of 22 children.

From 1947, West worked as a journalist, primarily writing for a small newspaper on Martha's Vineyard. In 1948, she started a weekly column about Oak Bluffs people, events, and nature. In 1982, The Feminist Press brought The Living Is Easy back into print, giving new attention to West and her role in the Harlem Renaissance and she was included in the 1992 anthology *Daughters of Africa* (ed. Margaret Busby). As a result of this renewed attention, at the age of 85 West finally finished a second novel, entitled *The Wedding*. Though its action occurs over the course of a weekend on Martha's Vineyard, it recounts the history of an affluent Black family over centuries. She dedicated it to Jacqueline Kennedy Onassis, who late in life was an editor at West's publisher, Doubleday, and who had encouraged her to complete it. Published to acclaim in 1995, the Publishers Weekly review stated: "West's first novel in 45 years is a triumph. Oprah Winfrey's production company turned the novel into two-part television miniseries, *The Wedding* in 1998. She wanted her legacy to be, "That I hung in there. That I didn't say I can't."

Gilbert Haven (September 19, 1821 – January 3, 1880) was a bishop of the Methodist Episcopal Church, elected in 1872. He was consecrated a bishop on May 24, 1872 at the Brooklyn Academy of Music in New York. He was an early benefactor of Clark College (now Clark Atlanta University), visualizing it as a university of all the Methodist schools founded for the education of freedmen (former African American slaves). He succeeded Bishop Davis Wasgatt Clark (for whom Clark College was named) as the President of the Freedman's Aid Society of the Methodist Episcopal Church. Bishop Gilbert Haven hosted President Ulysses S. Grant at his cottage on Clinton Avenue in the Campgrounds on the President's visit to Oak Bluffs. The plaque noting the visit can be seen today on the cottage.

Herbert E Tucker's career as a jurist began in 1973, when he was appointed special justice in the Dorchester District Court. He later became an associate justice in that court and in 1980 became the first Black justice in the Edgartown District Court, which he served until his retirement.

Stephen Lisle Carter (born October 26, 1954) is an American law professor at Yale University, legal- and social-policy writer, columnist, and best-selling novelist. Carter's non-fiction books have received praise from voices across the political spectrum, from Marion Wright Edelman to John Joseph O'Connor. Carter's first novel, *The Emperor of Ocean Park*, spent 11 weeks on the New York Times best-seller list in 2002.

Charles and Henrietta Shearer, who lived in Everett, Massachusetts, spent some of the summer on Martha's Vineyard in the Highlands. They decided to spend the full summer on the Island but needed additional income to afford the expense. With that goal in mind, Henrietta Shearer built a one story structure beside their house and opened a laundry. Her laundry was so successful that in 1912 they built a 12-room home on their property and opened an Inn for summer Black visitors called the Shearer Inn. She continued to run the laundry until her death in 1917.

Vernon Eulion Jordan Jr. (August 15, 1935 – March 1, 2021) was an American business executive and civil rights attorney who worked for various civil rights movement organizations before becoming a close advisor to President Bill Clinton.

Do You Know Oak Bluffs?

Wesleyan Grove is a 34-acre parcel of land in Oak Bluffs. Also known as the Martha's Vineyard Camp Meeting Association (MVCMA) or the "Campgrounds," it was the first summer religious camp established in the United States. It is famous for colorful cottages in a style now described as Carpenter Gothic. Today there are 318 cottages in the Campgrounds. Tents erected during the 1830's were later replaced by cottages in the 1850's and 1860's.

The open-air **Tabernacle** in the Campgrounds is made of cast iron, with seating for over 2,000. It is the physical and spiritual center of the Campground. It was built in 1879 by John W. Hoyt of Springfield, Massachusetts. Church services are held weekly in the Tabernacle during the months of July and August, and a variety of cultural events are held there each summer. Architecturally, the Tabernacle is a unique structure, with wrought iron arches and supports, two clerestories with dozens of colored glass windows, and an octagonal cupola.

Highland Wharf was built in 1871 by the Methodists so they would not have to disembark at the Oak Bluffs Wharf and pass through the temptations offered in that "unholy" summer resort. A horse-drawn trolley ran from the Highland Wharf directly into the Campground, delivering the faithful unsullied.

The first president to visit Martha's Vineyard was **President Grant** in March 1874, where he enjoyed a fireworks display, on Illumination Night, and the adoration of thousands.

Oak Bluffs has been a historically important center of **African American culture** since the eighteenth century. In 1907, the Town of Oak Bluffs changed its name from Cottage City to Oak Bluffs. Oak Bluffs was the only one of the six towns on the island to be consciously planned, and the only one developed specifically with tourism in mind.

The "Inkwell" or **Town Beach in Oak Bluffs** is the name of the popular beach frequented by African Americans beginning in the late nineteenth century. The strand was pejoratively called "The Inkwell" by nearby whites in reference to the skin color of the beachgoers. It is the most famous of beaches across the U.S. to transform this odious nickname into an emblem of pride.

Women made up most of the first **African American entrepreneurs** and played a pivotal role in attracting and accommodating the growing number of black visitors to the Island.

Shearer Cottage, founded by **Charles and Henrietta Shearer** in 1912 as a summer inn, began as a laundry operated by Henrietta which opened in 1903. The Cottage is the oldest and most well-known of these establishments that catered specifically to African Americans. Their daughters, granddaughters, and great granddaughters have continued management of the family's guest house into the twenty-first century.

President Barack Obama and his family are the most famous recent vacationers. They stayed in Oak Bluffs for their summer vacation in 2009, 2010, and 2011.

The **Flying Horses Carousel** is the country's oldest platform carousel, having been built back in 1876. It was originally an amusement at New York's Coney Island, but it was moved into a red barn on the island in 1884.

Ocean Park was originally laid out for house lots, but it was thought it would better be used as a community park. Back in the day, there were tennis courts on it. Now it is used for the spectacular fireworks display that usually falls on the third Friday in August. There is a home on Ocean Park in Oak Bluffs that has Cyrillic letters, which translate to "Dacha Peterhof." Dacha means "second home" in Russian. The letters are on the top front of the house. The home belongs to **Peter Norton,** computer-software publisher, author, and philanthropist, and founder of Norton Software.

The **double doors** on the front of the typical Queen Anne house in the Campgrounds mimic the central opening flaps of the tents they replaced.

Spike Lee's *Do the Right Thing* movie had one of its first showings at a makeshift drive-in in Oak Bluffs in the YMCA parking lot. The audio of the film was broadcast over an FM frequency.

In 1997, **Shearer Cottage** was the first landmark to be designated on the newly conceived African American Heritage Trail of Martha's Vineyard.

The area today known as **East Chop** was previously known as The Highlands.

Senator Edward W. Brooke, the first black U.S. Senator since the Reconstruction era, taught swimming at the Inkwell when he was on the Island.

In the 1950's, the beach between the **Steamship Authority Terminal** and the end of the stretch of sand was divided into three beaches. On the left was the "pay beach," which cost ten cents and gave the attendee access to bath houses, a pier and diving board, public rest rooms, lockers, showers, and a large concession stand. Next, separated by a fence was known as the "White Beach" and the third, separated by a pier was the **"Black Beach."** Both the White Beach and the Black beach designations were so identified by custom not by regulation.

Tivoli Day hits Oak Bluffs in September; it is always a wonderful time. It is a street festival with street vendors, live music, and food! There is also a parade of sorts in the evening, a live band that marches through town and collects people as it goes.

There is a **Cottage City Historic District Commission (CCHDC)** that reviews building projects in the district. It is the mission of the volunteer members of this Commission to act as stewards of our Victorian buildings and the unique architectural heritage of our seaside resort. It is expected that plans for any architectural changes visible from a public way will be presented to the CCHDC for review regarding adherence to historic architectural guidelines.

Martha's Vineyard African American Film Festival takes place in Oak Bluffs in the middle of August. In its twentieth year, it has grown in stature, and it is now the place that brings together Hollywood and Black actors and creative types.

The African American Heritage Trail of Martha's Vineyard is a compilation of many different sites dedicated to previously unrecognized contributions made by people of African heritage, to the island of Martha's Vineyard. Every site has a commemorative plaque describing each contribution. For several years, the history classes at the Martha's Vineyard Regional High School were involved as research assistants in the work of the Trail and acted as tour guides, site maintenance staff, mural painters, website developers, and musicians.

The first African-Americans to arrive on the Island in 1787 are believed to have been transported by John Saunders and his wife. They were formerly enslaved people who purchased their freedom in Virginia and traveled to Holmes Hole. John, being an exhorter, preached occasionally to the people of color at "Farm Neck." There is a rock in the

Farm Neck area known as Pulpit Rock where the preacher stood to exhort and spread the word of God.

The **Gazebo in Ocean Park** is one of the most iconic features of the town. Constructed in 1883, it stands tall on Circuit Avenue and provides a picturesque backdrop for visitors to enjoy views of the harbor and its surroundings. The gazebo has been a popular spot for locals.

Standing at 30 feet tall (two stories high), the gazebo's octagonal design features intricate lattice work and wooden spindles, which are illuminated with various lights during special occasions or holidays.

The gazebo has become a local landmark over the decades as residents and tourists alike flock to admire its aesthetic beauty. The iconic structure is also popular amongst photographers who come to capture picturesque scenes of the harbor or of people standing atop it with the backdrop of Martha's Vineyard in the distance. In addition to being an awe-inspiring sight to behold, the gazebo serves as a reminder of Oak Bluffs' history and culture as one of Massachusetts' most beloved summer destinations.

Not only is it a landmark feature in this quaint town but it also serves as an important part of its community. From jazz concerts on Circuit Avenue to family picnics beneath its shade - locals can often be found spending time at this wonderful place throughout the summer season. The gazebo's presence is not only symbolic but actively contributes to creating memories both for those who call Oak Bluffs home and those who visit for just a short while each year.

A six-foot-tall zinc figure of a Union Soldier perched on a cast iron fountain base was presented as a gift to the town of Oak Bluffs by **Charles Strahan**, a former lieutenant in the Confederate Army who relocated to Martha's Vineyard in 1891.

The stock statue was manufactured by J. W. Fiske of New York City. After its original installation in the Village Square it was moved twice, before settling at its current location in Ocean Park. The figure is also reported to have toppled during a hurricane over fifty years ago.

All About Tisbury/Vineyard Haven

Tisbury is a town located on Martha's Vineyard with a population of 4,815 at the 2020 census. Vineyard Haven is the main village/town center of Tisbury. The two names are used interchangeably. As can be seen in the history section below, the town of Tisbury was incorporated within the Commonwealth of Massachusetts in 1671 and remains the legal name of the town to this day. However, the port and harbor have had varying names. "Holmes Hole" was one of the first names of the port within the town of Tisbury. This name was later changed to "Vineyard Haven", which is the official post office name for the community. To residents of Martha's Vineyard, "Vineyard Haven" is by far the more common usage, although residents recognize Tisbury as the town's legal name.

The area was called "Nobnocket" by the Wampanoag people and was first referred to by the colonial settlers as "Homes Hole," "Homes" from a Wampanoag term for "old man" and "Hole" meaning a sheltered inlet. By the 19th century, it was more commonly spelled "Holmes Hole" after the descendants of John Holmes (1730–1812) who had settled in the village during the second half of the 18th century. The village officially changed its name to Vineyard Haven in 1871. The name Vineyard Haven technically refers only to one section of the town of Tisbury, but the names are used interchangeably and Vineyard Haven is commonly used as a title for the whole town.

Vineyard Haven is the main port of entry to Martha's Vineyard and one of the three main population centers (along with Edgartown and Oak Bluffs). The Steamship Authority wharf, located in Vineyard Haven, is where ferries arrive and depart year-round. (A second, seasonal wharf is located in neighboring Oak Bluffs.) The year-round population is only about 2,000 people, but that number increases tremendously in the summer.

51

The Wampanoag have lived on Martha's Vineyard, which they called Noepe, continuously for approximately 5,000-15,000 years. The first English maritime explorer, Bartholomew Gosnold, came in 1602. Six decades later, in 1660, Tisbury was first settled by James Allen, William Peabody and Lt. Josiah Standish, a son of Captain Myles Standish. It was officially incorporated in 1671 by Francis Lovelace, Governor General of New York. The town, which originally included the lands of West Tisbury, was named for Tisbury, Wiltshire, England, the hometown of Martha's Vineyard Governor Mayhew. Citizens of the island, unhappy with the leadership of Governor Mayhew, petitioned William III and Mary II in 1673 for a change of leadership, and the entire island, including the town, became a part of Massachusetts. The town was divided into its current boundaries in 1892.

The town has long thrived on the sea and is now the home of the main ferry docks for the island. The island's first and primary ferry line is the Steamship Authority, which runs to and from Woods Hole, New Bedford, and Nantucket (in the summer months from the Oak Bluffs terminal), all in Massachusetts. There are several other private ferry lines that serve Martha's Vineyard as well, with terminals in the towns of Oak Bluffs and Edgartown.

To get an idea of the embarkation in summer of passengers – tourists primarily – and goods, see the early scene in the movie Jaws which shows the debarkation on "Amity Island" of a typical boatload in summer at the Vineyard Haven Steamship Authority facility from the steamship Naushon. At the time of the filming of Jaws in 1975, this was the largest of the ferries, running only in the summer months for its high passenger capacity. It ceased service in 1987 and has been replaced by more modern vessels.

People of Significance – Tisbury/Vineyard Haven

The first white settler to live at Vineyard Haven was **Francis Usselton**, about 1660. He was forced to leave because he had made secret purchases from the Indians without the consent of Governor Mayhew. Usselton went to Newport, Rhode Island. **Huzzelton's Head** in Tisbury perpetuates his name.

After her husband died, **Katherine Cornell** decided to retire from the stage altogether. She sold her residences and bought a house on East 51st Street in Manhattan, and she also bought an old building on Martha's Vineyard known as The Barn and made additions to it, and restored the 300-year-old Association Hall on the island.

The **Tisbury Town Hall** on Martha's Vineyard houses a theater on its second floor. Originally known as Association Hall, it was renamed **"The Katharine Cornell Theater"** in her honor and later, her memory. A donation from her estate provided the funds for renovation (lighting, heating, elevator) as well as decoration of four large murals depicting Vineyard life and legend by local artist Stan Murphy. The Katharine Cornell Theater is a popular venue for plays, music, movies and more. Her gravesite and memorial are located next door to the Theater.

The early history of Vineyard Haven centers around its old taverns. In 1677-78, **Lieutenant Isaac Chase** kept a public house. The "Great House" was built by his grandson Abraham Chase about 1720 and was the center of village life for more than a century. Many interesting stories cluster around this house and its occupants of the olden days.

The first Methodist preacher on the island was **Rev. Jesse Lee**, the founder of Methodism in the Northern States. He preached the first sermon at the Proprietors' Meeting House, February 4, 1795. The society was formed and incorporated March 7, 1833, as the First Methodist Episcopal Society. They soon erected the building on Church Street now known as **Capawock Hall**, owned by the Masonic order.

In the month of August, 1913, the people of Vineyard Haven gave a most interesting historical pageant of Martha's Vineyard, under the leadership of **Mrs. Barbara S. Look**, on the shores of Lake Tashmoo. A cast of more than a hundred and fifty people presented the following scenes from the island history: I. The Pawwaws, 1600; II. Gosnold's Visit to the Island, 1602; III. The Stealing of Epenow by Captain Hunt, 1614; IV. The Place on the Wayside, 1657; V. The Purchase of Homses Hole, 1664; VI. Grey's Raid, 1778, and the Liberty Pole. The principal actors were in most cases direct descendants of the persons they represented, and many of the costumes and properties were family heirlooms. This pageant was a great success in every way and will long be remembered.

Do You Know Tisbury/Vineyard Haven?

Vineyard Haven is a community within the Town of Tisbury. The first white settler to live at Vineyard Haven was Francis Usselton, about 1660. He was forced to leave because he had made secret purchases from the Indians without the consent of Governor Mayhew. Usselton went to Newport, Rhode Island. Huzzelton's Head in Tisbury perpetuates his name.

Tisbury and Edgartown are the two original towns on the Island.

Holmes Hole was the original name for Vineyard Haven and at the turn of the nineteenth century, it saw more traffic than Edgartown Harbor.

The current forty-five-foot **West Chop** lighthouse was constructed in 1891. The West Chop characteristic is an occulting white light of four second intervals. An occulting light is a rhythmic light in which the duration of light is longer than the duration of darkness. It is, in effect, the opposite of a flashing light.

Long called the **Mansion House**, the name it bears today, the inn dates to 1769 and has been ravaged by fire more than once over the centuries. The current building went up in the 1880s, changing hands, names, and decorative schemes repeatedly during the 20th century.

One great bit of local Martha's Vineyard knowledge is a hidden location for kayakers to easily put their kayaks into **Lake Tashmoo**. Tucked away down a long dirt road on the western side of Vineyard Haven's beautiful Lake Tashmoo is a small Landbank property with an even smaller beach and, more importantly, a kayak launch. There is limited parking for six cars, but usually there are open spaces.

The Island blocked McDonald's from coming to Vineyard Haven in the famous 1978 **Sack the Mac** campaign.

The **Sailors' Burial Ground** is the last resting place of seventy-six seafarers, who either passed away at the old Marine Hospital (now the Martha's Vineyard Museum) or who died on ships whilst at port on Martha's Vineyard. All seventy-six of those buried here are from off-island and the majority were from countries across the ocean, Norway, England, Scotland, Denmark, Cape Verde, Finland and Holland.

Tisbury Meadow Preserve in Vineyard Haven is a wonderfully pristine "Down-Island" hiking trail that is hidden in plain sight. It is an 84-acre MV Land Bank property with a trailhead located directly on State Road between the "Down-Island" turning on to Lambert's Cove Road and the Scottish Bakehouse (on the left-hand side if you are traveling in an "Up-Island" direction).

In 1923, the **Catboat** was built in Edgartown. **Manuel Swartz Roberts** constructed it in what is now the Old Sculpin Gallery on the waterfront. This beautifully restored twenty-two foot vessel was once a workboat used for fishing, scalloping, and summer charters.

The **Vanity** is a catboat owned by the Martha's Vineyard Museum. In keeping with true Catboat design, she is half as wide as she is long, providing a very stable working and sailing platform.

During the Revolution, this harbor was the refuge for many British men-of-war. In 1775 the people of Holmes Hole erected a **"liberty pole"** on Manter's Hill. As another expression of public feeling the women threw all their tea into the hole to show their attitude regarding the Boston Port Bill.

55

Holmes Hole did her part in the **Civil War** by sending eighty-seven men into the army and twenty into the navy.

The town of **Tisbury** was once known as a prominent whaling station. Many of the town's historic buildings were **destroyed by fire** in 1833 but there are several historic homes that still overlook the harbor on William Street.

Vineyard Haven is home to the oldest working cinema in Massachusetts. **The Capawock Theater** was built in 1913 and restored extensively in 2015. The cinema regularly runs limited arthouse films and rep classics programmed by the Martha Vineyard's Film Society. Every summer they host a week-long, Jaws-inspired shark-themed film festival as well as weekly screenings of the Spielberg classic.

Martha's Vineyard Family Campground is the only campground on Martha's Vineyard, and it specializes in making all that the Island offers both accessible and affordable to all camping families. Located just one and a half miles from the Vineyard Haven ferry terminal, it offers spacious wooded sites, complete with picnic tables, fireplaces, and hookups to accommodate tents or RVs. It also offers a number of new camping cabin rentals. Other amenities include modern restrooms with hot showers, laundromat, store, recreation hall and playground.

West Chop Light is a lighthouse station located at the entrance of Vineyard Haven Harbor in Tisbury on the northern tip of West Chop, a few miles from the village of Vineyard Haven.

The first 25-foot rubblestone lighthouse and dwelling were built on the bluffs of West Chop in 1817. Following constant erosion, the lighthouse was moved back in 1830, and again in 1846.

The present 45-foot tall brick tower and dwelling were built in 1891. In 1976 West Chop Light became the last Martha's Vineyard lighthouse to be automated, but the original Fresnel lens is still in operation.

All About West Tisbury

West Tisbury is a town located on Martha's Vineyard with a population of 3,555 at the 2020 census.

West Tisbury was first settled by English settlers in 1669 as part of the town of Tisbury. The town, officially incorporated in 1892, was the last town on Martha's Vineyard to be incorporated. Despite its separation from Tisbury, the original settlement of the town is still located in West Tisbury. Historically, it has been the agricultural heartland of the island. Up through the 1980s West Tisbury was one of the quickest growing communities on the island.

Along with Chilmark and Aquinnah, West Tisbury forms "Up-Island" Martha's Vineyard.

The town has long thrived on the sea and is now the home of the main ferry docks for the island. The island's first and primary ferry line is the Steamship Authority, which runs to and from Woods Hole, New Bedford, and Nantucket (in the summer months from the Oak Bluffs terminal), all in Massachusetts. There are several other private ferry lines that serve Martha's Vineyard as well, with terminals in the towns of Oak Bluffs and Edgartown.

People of Significance – West Tisbury

Nancy Luce was orphaned by her parents, Philip Luce and Anne Manter, in her late twenties and suffered a debilitating disease leaving her nearly homebound at the family farmhouse. She raised bantam hens to survive, often giving them fanciful names such as Ottee Ophete, Pondy Lilly and Letoogie Tickling. She wrote and self-published poetry pamphlets about her chickens and got professional portraits done of them and herself.

Tourists would come to her cottage and small store on the property to visit with her and purchase keepsakes to bring home. As she buried her chickens on the property, her collection of chicken gravestones became its own tourist attraction. She was considered "one of the Island's most well-known historical figures."

When Luce died, the chicken gravestones were given to the town library. Luce herself is buried in the West Tisbury cemetery, where her marble gravestone is decorated with chickens.

Willy Mason was born in White Plains, New York, the son of Jemima James and Michael Mason, both songwriters. Mason is a direct descendant of the 19th-century philosopher William James, the brother of novelist Henry James.

When Mason was five, he and his family moved from Tarrytown, New York to West Tisbury, Massachusetts, on the island of Martha's Vineyard.

He attended Chilmark Elementary School through 5th grade, West Tisbury Elementary School and Martha's Vineyard Regional High School, where he participated in several local bands such as Keep Thinking, Cultivation, and Slow Leslie. He also was in the MVRHS Minnesingers and performed in musical theater productions.

Do You Know – West Tisbury?

Horticulturist Polly Hill developed the Polly Hill Arboretum on her 20-acre property over the past 40 years and allows the public to wander the grounds. Wanderers will pass old stone walls on the way to the Tunnel of Love, an arbor of bleached hornbeam. There are also witch hazels, camellias, magnolias, and rhododendrons.

Upper Lambert's Cove begins in the center of West Tisbury and accesses Lambert's Cove Beach, Seth's Pond and the *FOCUS* Study Center. It is the sole access to many summer and year-round residences.

One finds scenes of waves beating against boulders at Cedar Tree Neck Sanctuary, the Obed Sherman Daggett and Maria Roberts Daggett Sanctuary, the A.S. Reed Bird Refuge, Fish Hook and the George A. Hough Preserve – properties collectively known as **Cedar Tree Neck Sanctuary**. One also finds excellent examples of the habitats and vistas that make Martha's Vineyard such a special place. A one-time visitor here can get a sense of the varied natural endowment of the Vineyard; a seasoned naturalist could spend a lifetime pursuing the secrets of the Sanctuary's diverse flora and fauna.

The position of **Poet Laureate** of West Tisbury officially came into being on April 11, 2006, by a voice vote at the West Tisbury Annual Town Meeting. Soon afterwards, at the recommendation of an advisory committee formed by the West Tisbury Library, the Selectmen appointed Daniel Waters the town's first Poet Laureate

The Field Gallery, on State Road, offers a comfortable, supportive, ever-changing exhibition environment, featuring contemporary art by both emerging and established artists. Founded in 1970, the gallery hosts three spaces with rotating exhibits of paintings, sculpture, photography, jewelry, and more. Outside, the large field is home to the whimsical sculptures of Field Gallery founder Tom Maley and many others.

Question: Where is this church located and what is its name?

Answer on page 61

The Treasures of Martha's Vineyard

I define "Treasures" as the places, institutions, and organizations that make Martha's Vineyard an incredibly special place for thousands of people. Some are well known, and others are best known by full and part time residents. I have selected the ones that, to me, and hopefully to the reader, qualify as special. After you have experienced them, you feel a sense of admiration and wonder. People who live on or visit Martha's Vineyard are indeed fortunate to experience these incredibly special organizations, places, and institutions.

Wesleyan Grove – The Campgrounds

Wesleyan Grove is a 34-acre National Historic Landmark District in Oak Bluffs. Also known as the Martha's Vineyard Camp Meeting Association (MVCMA) or the Campgrounds, it was the first summer religious camp established in the United States. It is famous for its approximately 300 colorful cottages in a style now described as Carpenter Gothic.

Just after the American Civil War, the area developed as a large Methodist summer campground with open air Christian revivals. This meeting style became popular around the United States at the time, Colorful, ornate, gingerbread cottages were built in an oak grove around a central church tabernacle.

The grove was added to the National Register of Historic Places in 1978, recognized in 2000 by the National Trust for Historic Preservation and declared a National Historic Landmark by the US Department of the Interior in 2005. The first so-called camp meeting in what became known as Wesleyan Grove was held in 1835. Over subsequent years, participants began arriving early and staying after the revival. Nine tents

Answer from page 60: It is located in Tisbury and is
the First Congregational Church of West Tisbury.

provided shelter for the first campers in 1835, but as the campers grew in number, families chose to pitch tents of their own; there were one hundred tents in 1851 and that increased to 320 by 1858, located around the preaching ground.

In subsequent years, the congregations grew enormously, and many of the thousands in attendance were housed in large tents known as "society tents." A congregation from a church on the mainland would maintain its own society tent. Conditions were cramped, with men and women sleeping dormitory-style on opposite sides of a central canvas divider. Society tents were arranged in a semicircle on Trinity Park.

Over time, families began leasing small lots on which to pitch their own individual tents. "Between 1855 and 1865 the camp meetings began to change in character. They continued to be religious in nature, but the participants also began to enjoy the benefit of the sea air and social interaction as they revived both mind and body."

Today the Campground is a community of summer residents and a smaller number of year-round residents who own the cottages (often fully modernized) or rent them from the owners. Some of these folks are descendants of early revivalists although Wesleyan Grove is no longer a revivalist camp. Sunday services are still held in the summer, but the Grove has been non-denominational since the 1930s. Nonetheless, a Grand Illumination takes place on a Wednesday evening in summer (Illumination Night), with illuminated paper or silk lanterns, continuing a 150-year tradition.

The open-air Tabernacle, made of cast iron, with seating for over 2,000, is the physical and spiritual center of the Campground. It was built in 1879. Church services are held weekly in the Tabernacle during the months of July and August, and a variety of cultural events are held there each summer.

The first event of the season is the graduation ceremonies of the Martha's Vineyard Regional High School. Architecturally, the Tabernacle is a unique structure, with wrought iron arches and supports, two clerestories with dozens of colored glass windows, and an octagonal cupola. The Tabernacle was completely restored in 2019.

Gay Head – Aquinnah Cliffs and Lighthouse

The Gay Head Cliffs are a national landmark. The beautiful, colorful layers of clay make up the cliffs. It has been said that fossil bones of whales, camels and wild horses have been found in the cliff layers. The Gay Head Lighthouse is perched atop the cliffs. It is the only working lighthouse on Martha's Vineyard.

In 1796, Massachusetts State Senator, Peleg Coffin, requested a lighthouse be installed on Martha's Vineyard above the Gay Head cliffs overlooking a dangerous section of underwater rocks known as "Devil's Bridge." Senator Peleg's request to his Congressman in Washington was substantiated by the maritime traffic navigating the waters between Gay Head and the Elizabeth Islands, which would eventually be reported in a late 1800s Massachusetts study at 80,000 vessels annually.

As the state representative for Nantucket, Peleg Coffin also had the whaling industry interests of Nantucket in mind. The Gay Head lighthouse was authorized in 1798 by the United States Congress during the Presidency of John Adams. This authorization was to help facilitate safe passage for vessels passing through the hazardous Vineyard Sound waters near the Gay Head cliffs.

The existing fifty-one feet tall conical brick tower that stands today was started in 1854 and lit in 1856. The bricks used to construct the light were composed of clay bricks manufactured at the nine-mile distant Chilmark brickyard. It was equipped with a whale oil fired first-order Fresnel Lens standing about 12 feet tall; weighing several tons; and containing 1,008 hand-made crystal prisms.

In 2015 the Lighthouse was moved to its current location. The new location of the Gay Head Light is approximately 180 feet back from the eroding cliff's face. It has been estimated by engaged geologists that the lighthouse will not be threatened again for another 150 years.

Melissa Bigelow

The Shearer Inn

In 1912, Charles Shearer, a son of a slave and her white owner, turned one of the cottages in Oak Bluffs into the very first inn for black vacationers.

In the late 1890's he purchased a cottage in the Highlands of East Chop. At the time Oak Bluffs was the only town where African-Americans could purchase property.

He capitalized on the human feeling of wanting a safe place for African – Americans to spend their vacation time on the Vineyard. He founded the Shearer Inn and soon Oak Bluffs began to attract well to do African Americans from all over the country.

In 1912 the Shearer Cottage started to receive paying guests and thrived. The Inn prospered, more rooms, a new kitchen, and a dining room were added. A tennis court was built in the backyard.

Most of the guests in the early years were from Boston and other Massachusetts cities. Whenever the inn was fully booked, the Shearers beseeched neighboring friends to accommodate overflow guests in their home.

Word spread to New York. Guests of distinction included James S. Watson, one of the state's first black judges; Bishop "Sweet Daddy" Grace; actress-singer Ethel Waters; beauty magnate Madam C.J. Walker; opera soloist Lillian Evanti; and singer Roland B. Hayes.

In the 1970s, Lionel Richie and the Commodores stayed at Shearer Cottage on occasion. Their manager was a Shearer grandson. During their stay, the fledgling recording group honed their act in Island clubs and even once on South Beach.

Many of the guests bought their own summer homes in Oak Bluffs. Today's Shearer Cottage attracts guests from across racial and international lines and serves as a popular venue for private events – especially when the occasions hold resonance for black history or culture.

The Flying Horses

The Flying Horses Carousel is the oldest operating platform carousel in America. Located in Oak Bluffs, the carousel was apparently first located in New York City before being moved to the island in the 1880s.

The carousel was listed on the National Register of Historic Places in 1979 and designated a National Historic Landmark in 1987. The carousel is one of only a handful of carousels that still have brass rings for a rider to attempt to grab as the carousel rotates. Since being moved to the island, it has been housed in a somewhat utilitarian single-story building. It is sheathed in wood shingles and has a low gable roof.

Despite the name "Flying Horses," the horses are stationary when the carousel is rotating. The horses have their original oxide eyes, but their original horsehair manes have been lost.

The layout of the horses and carriages is as follows: a chariot, two pairs of horses, a chariot, three pairs of horses, and then the entire sequence repeated. The panels that decorate the carousel, including those surrounding the central column housing the carousel machinery, depict equestrian and marine scenes. By the 1980s, these panels, needing restoration, were removed and replaced by panels of local scenes done by a local artist. When the site was purchased by the Martha's Vineyard Land Trust, the Flying Horses underwent an extensive restoration, returning the carousel to its original appearance, complete with the historic panel paintings that were done by a Dare Company artist.

Although originally powered by steam, the carousel was converted to electricity in 1900, and is powered by a 10-horsepower motor located in the building's basement. The gears and belts connecting the motor to the carousel were rehabilitated in the 1980s. The ride has a traditional ring assembly, where the lucky rider who successfully grabs a brass ring gets a free ride.

The carousel's music is provided by a 1923 Wurlitzer #103 Band Organ.

Melissa Bigelow

Martha's Vineyard Museum

The Martha's Vineyard Museum is the Island's largest repository of cultural artifacts, historic photographs, archival records, and genealogical records. The mission of The Martha's Vineyard Museum is to inspire all people to discover, explore, and strengthen their connections to this Island and its diverse heritage.

The Martha's Vineyard Museum was originally known as the Dukes County Historical Society. It was founded in 1922 and incorporated the following year. The founders first acquired revolutionary era documents, which started the collection. They devoted a great deal of their time, energy, and resources towards the documentation of the Island's role in American history and greater maritime industry.

The Society signed a long-term lease agreement with the Coast Guard to steward the Edgartown, East Chop, and Gay Head Lighthouses in 1992. The agreement is still in place for the East Chop and Edgartown Lighthouses. The Town of Aquinnah assumed stewardship of the Gay Head Light in summer 2018 when ownership transferred from the Coast Guard. Portions of the original Museum campus in Edgartown were sold as part of the move to Vineyard Haven, but the Museum maintains ownership of the historic Cooke House and the surrounding property. The grounds have been transformed into beautiful gardens to create the Cooke House and Legacy Gardens.

It is currently the newly renovated museum, moved from Edgartown to Vineyard Haven in 2018, taking over the former 1895 Marine Hospital. This world-class museum offers visitors a variety of rotating exhibits and permanent collections for viewing. Its main exhibit is called "One Island – Many Stories" found on the main floor. But perhaps its most unique feature is the glass pavilion anchored by an enormous Fresnel Lens. This is the original 1856 lens from the Gay Head Lighthouse.

While there is much to admire inside, a walk amongst the manicured grounds is a true treat as well. The museum sits on a bluff overlooking Lagoon Pond and Vineyard Sound in Tisbury for some of the best views on the island.

South Beach

South Beach runs the entire length of the southern end of Martha's Vineyard; however, the name "South Beach" commonly refers to a stretch of public beach that is demarcated by Herring Creek Road on the west and Chappaquiddick Island on the east. The name Norton Point is given to the stretch of beach that runs from Katama Road to Wasque Point, the southeastern most point of the beach on Chappaquiddick.

Situated in the southern end of Edgartown, South Beach is a three-mile barrier beach. It is one of the most popular public beaches in Martha's Vineyard, largely because of its rugged surf on the Atlantic Oceanside. Aside from being a surfer's paradise, the beach is easily accessible from Edgartown by bike which eliminates the hassle of finding parking on busy days.

The Polly Hill Arboretum

The Polly Hill Arboretum includes 20 acres under cultivation, with an additional 40 acres of native woodland, located on Martha's Vineyard at 809 State Road, West Tisbury. It has been developed since 1958 by the horticulturist Polly Hill, and was listed on the National Register of Historic Places in 2015.

In 1687, Henry Luce, one of the first English settlers on Martha's Vineyard purchased four hundred acres of land in the island's center from the natives. In 1926, 40 acres of this land, then a sheep farm, were acquired by Hill's family. After his father's death, Hill decided to create an arboretum in 1958, growing the trees from seed. Through purchase of adjacent land, the property was increased to a total of sixty acres. The Arboretum's administrative offices are housed in a building dating from the 1670s. Other historic structures on the property include the Far Barn (circa 1750) with its attached Slaughterhouse, the Cow Barn (a private residence), and the adjacent "Gym."

The Arboretum now contains North Tisbury azaleas, witch-hazels, winter hazels, camellias, magnolias, stuartias, conifers, and deciduous and evergreen hollies, and incorporates a dogwood avenue and a pleached hornbeam arbor. Polly Hill plant introductions include varieties of Cornus kousa, Ilex, Stewartia, and about forty Rhododendrons.

Chappaquiddick Island

Norton Point, a narrow barrier beach, connects Martha's Vineyard and Chappaquiddick between Katama and Wasque (pronounced way-sqwee). Occasional breaches occur due to hurricanes and strong storms separating the islands for periods of time. Most recently, the two were separated for 8 years from 2007 to 2015.

Visitors come to the isolated island for beaches, cycling, hiking, nature tours and birding, as well as the MyToi Gardens, a small Japanese garden created amidst the native brush. Two fire trucks are stationed on the island from Edgartown. Chappaquiddick Road and Poucha Road, both paved, provide access to sandy, woodland roads, trails, and shorelines.

Menemsha

Menemsha is a small fishing village located in the town of Chilmark on the island of Martha's Vineyard in Dukes County. It is located on the east coast of Menemsha Pond, adjacent to the opening into the Vineyard Sound on the pond's northern end. The village's historic harbor serves as the point of departure for local fishermen, some from multi-generational fishing families, as well as charter boats to the Elizabeth Islands and elsewhere. Besides charter fishing and cruises, other amenities are the public beach adjacent to the harbor and the bicycle ferry across Menemsha Pond to Aquinnah. Menemsha is the location of a United States Coast Guard station, Coast Guard Station Menemsha, and was once known as Menemsha Creek.

It was the shooting background for the fictional "Amity Island" of Steven Spielberg's 1975 film Jaws.

Public Beaches

Menemsha Beach

Chilmark's Menemsha Beach is a popular sunset spot on the Vineyard, with many choosing to cap their day on this calm and quiet strip of sand by watching the sun gently sink into the sea across the Vineyard Sound. The waters at Menemsha tend to be calm, and the daily presence of lifeguards makes this beach a great choice for a relaxing swim. Plus, the seafood shacks near Menemsha Beach offer the perfect sunset snack!

Oak Bluffs Town Beach

Located in adorable Oak Bluffs, considered one of the best beach towns in New England and known for its antique Flying Horses Carousel and whimsical gingerbread cottage neighborhood, Oak Bluffs Town Beach is sometimes called Inkwell Beach. There are lifeguards present in the summer, a great sandbar for playing on, and its easy proximity to so many great places to stay and eat doesn't hurt its appeal, either!

Katama Beach

Also referred to as South Beach, Edgartown's Katama Beach is one of the best Martha's Vineyard beaches because it offers options for catching some waves on the Atlantic Ocean side, or playing in the calm waters of the protected pond on the other side of this barrier beach. Lifeguards patrol this 3+ mile beach during the swim season, but the undertow and currents are powerful on the ocean side, so keep that in mind when choosing where to take a dip!

Moshup Beach

Also known as Gay Head Beach, Moshup Beach is a fantastic Martha's Vineyard beach for scenic views, with the stunning Gay Head Cliffs providing a fantastic backdrop for the beach. There is a bit of a walk to get there from the parking lot, so be prepared. Lifeguards are not often present on Moshup Beach, and the surf can get intense, so this may not be the beach for those looking for calm waters. Sections of the beach here allow nude sunbathing.

Lake Tashmoo Town Beach

Another favorite Martha's Vineyard beach for families with kids is Tisbury's Lake Tashmoo Town Beach. It offers the option of swimming in the Vineyard Sound or in Lake Tashmoo, the protected waters on the other side of the beach. The presence of lifeguards and the gentle waters of Lake Tashmoo make this a great beach choice for younger children. The beach offers the options of swimming in the lake or in Vineyard Sound.

Long Point Beach

A part of Long Point Wildlife Refuge in West Tisbury, Long Point Beach is located in a naturalist's dream, with oak forest, savannah, wildflower meadows and more just waiting to be explored! There are no lifeguards on duty at the beach, but kayak and standup paddleboards are available for rent every summer, so for anyone who is looking for a beautiful beach experience beyond just sunbathing and catching the waves, Long Point Beach might be the Martha's Vineyard beach for you!

Joseph Sylvia State Beach

Edgartown's Joseph Sylvia State Beach is often shortened to just State Beach, and it is a favorite Martha's Vineyard beach for kids and adults alike! In addition to having smaller waves and lifeguards, it is also the site of the famous "Jaws Bridge," and kids and their adults enjoy climbing up and jumping off into the calm waters below!

East Beach

Just a quick ferry ride over to Chappaquiddick, East Beach is a great Vineyard beach for those looking for a quieter beach than some of the other popular Martha's Vineyard beaches! Enjoy a stroll on the soft sand, the Cape Poge Lighthouse views, and the sounds of the often-dramatic surf on this exposed side of the island. There are no lifeguards on East Beach, but it sure makes for a sweet romantic picnic spot!

Owen Park Beach

Tisbury's Owen Park Beach is always a hit with families, as it has ample facilities, a playground for the kiddos, the perfect spot to watch the ferry come and go, and calm water for the whole family to enjoy. This harbor beach is also close to great Martha's Vineyard places to stay and eat, like the famous Black Dog Tavern!

Lobsterville Beach

Beautiful Lobsterville Beach is another gorgeous Martha's Vineyard beach in Aquinnah, with mostly calm waters along its 2-mile shore; while it is open to the public, public parking is very limited. Lobsterville Beach is a great spot for swimming, but there is no lifeguard on duty, so it is not always a first choice for families with young kids. Snorkeling near the shore is a popular activity here!

Secret Beach

Secret Beach is also known as Great Rock Bight, and is located in Chilmark. The land is owned by the MV Landbank Commission so the land will never be built on, and is kept pristine for visitors. The best part of Great Rock Bight? The large boulder located just off shore that is perfect for climbing on to and jumping off of. To get there, travel on North Road up to Chilmark and turn right on to the old Brickyard Road. You're going to travel a ways through the woods to a wooded parking lot. Once you park, follow the path all the way down to the beach. Warning: Strollers aren't advisable for this path, and there are very steep wooden stairs you'll have to use to come and go from the beach.

Fishing

Martha's Vineyard has always been a popular destination for fishing and recreational activities, but in recent years the island has become known for its incredible opportunities for deep sea fishing. During the summer months, anglers flock to Martha's Vineyard in search of big game species such as tuna, marlin, swordfish, and mahi-mahi as well as smaller catches like pollock and redfish. Deep sea fishing requires specialized equipment, so it is important to hire a knowledgeable guide who can provide you with all the necessary gear. Once out at sea you will have the chance to explore some of the most beautiful parts of New England's coastlines while keeping an eye out for any potential catches!

No matter what your skill level or experience, there is plenty of fun to be had when fishing on Martha's Vineyard. Whether you want to try your luck at deep sea fishing or would prefer something more relaxing like surfcasting from shore or inshore trolling from a boat; either way you won't be disappointed by what this wonderful island has to offer!

In addition to being an excellent place for anglers looking to catch their dinner, Martha's Vineyard also provides visitors with unique cultural experiences related to its long history of fishing traditions. For centuries Native Americans conducted ceremonies involving burning juniper branches over open coals to ward off evil spirits and bring good luck - this practice is still carried out today in some parts of the island known as 'frailing'. Exploring these stories and rituals provides insight into the culture surrounding the island which many visitors find fascinating!

No trip would be complete without sampling some delicious seafood straight from Martha's Vineyard itself! Freshly caught fish can be found everywhere on the island from locals selling from their boats up at

Menemsha beach, right through to restaurants serving up an array of creative dishes featuring locally sourced ingredients including seafood chowder, lobster rolls, grilled squid salad and much more!

Whether you're a novice just looking for a relaxed day out on the water or an avid angler seeking that big catch; fishing on Martha's Vineyard offers something for everyone! From deep sea excursions filled with thrills and tales about mythical creatures protecting fishermen at sea; right down through quaint rituals like "frailing" - there are plenty of unforgettable experiences awaiting discovery!

World War II had been over for a year when a group of forward thinking fishermen came together to form an annual autumn tradition to promote Vineyard camaraderie and sportsmanship. The creation of the derby came at an ideal time, when the Island community was looking at expanding its tourist industry. In 1946 the idea, according to the late Al Brickman, was formulated by a public relations man named Nat Sperber, working for the new ferry service owned by Russell Stearns and Ralph Hornblower. His mission was to come up with a fall promotion. So began the **Martha's Vineyard Striped Bass and Blue Fish Derby.** The contest drew 1,000 fishermen from 29 states and as faraway as Ontario. Today's derby attracts fishermen from all around the world and participation in recent years has approached 2,000.

The Ferries

There's something about a destination that requires an ocean crossing. Whether for business or pleasure, the voyage itself is integral to the experience. The expectant faces of passengers embarking at the ferry terminal in Woods Hole, Massachusetts tell this story. The trip between Cape Cod and Martha's Vineyard may take only 45 minutes, but it's an adventure.

This is as true now as it was over a century ago, when predecessors of the Woods Hole, Martha's Vineyard and Nantucket Steamship Authority's modern fleet plied the waters between Massachusetts' coast and the islands. Over the years, dozens of commercial ships of various sizes and types transported passengers to Martha's Vineyard and Nantucket. Several that serviced Martha's Vineyard during the early 20th century bear mentioning here.

Among the early vessels on the Steamship Authority's "historic fleet" roster is the Uncatena. Named for one of the Elizabeth Islands and operating from 1902 to 1928, Uncatena was the first steel hull steamer built to serve Martha's Vineyard and the last side-wheel paddleboat to sail the route. The SS Islander (renamed the SS Martha's Vineyard in 1928) had a similarly long run, ferrying passengers to the Vineyard for 33 years until its sale to another steamship company in 1956.

Boasting an even longer stint was the Nobska, which operated for 48 years until its retirement in 1973. This ship's legacy endures – its whistle installed on a current Steamship Authority ferry, the MV Eagle, and a metal replica of it perched atop the Oak Bluffs ferry terminal.

Two of the former ferries saw battle in World War II. Operating the Martha's Vineyard route starting in 1928 and 1929, respectively, the New Bedford and the Naushon were requisitioned by the US War Shipping Administration in 1942 and both participated in the Invasion of Normandy.

74

Another vessel named Naushon made history too. Operating from 1957 to 1987 (initially as the SS Nantucket), this later Naushon was the last steam-powered ferry in regular operation on the East Coast.

These and others comprise a grand tradition of ferry service between the Massachusetts mainland and the islands – a legacy that continues today with the Steamship Authority's fleet of ten ships, seven of which sail the Martha's Vineyard route.

Sailing Around Martha's Vineyard – Do You Know?

If you want to experience the beauty of Martha's Vineyard from a different perspective, then sailing around its small islands is the perfect way to do it. From the lighthouses to the quaint fishing villages and historical sites on each island, there is no shortage of adventure awaiting those who take their sailboats out into the waters.

One of the best places to begin your journey is Oak Bluffs, where you can launch your vessel from East Chop Beach and sail off into the sunset. Enjoy taking in all of the scenery as you make your way towards Menemsha Harbor for one of the most stunning sunsets imaginable. As you navigate through this protected area, be sure to look for pinnipeds such as harbor seals, grey seals, and sometimes even humpback whales just waiting to be spotted!

Once you reach Aquinnah at the western tip of Martha's Vineyard, take some time to explore some of its unique attractions like exploring clay cliffs and meandering walkways tucked away near its famous Gay Head Cliffs. Or if you're feeling up to a more daring adventure - hop aboard a kiteboard or stand-up paddleboard while making your way around this picturesque island!

The Best Nature Walks on Martha's Vineyard

Martha's Vineyard is home to some of the most breathtaking natural scenery in New England - and there are plenty of ways to explore it! Here are some of the best nature walks to go on during your visit:

Felix Neck Wildlife Sanctuary: This 4-mile loop trail will take you through a variety of habitats, from beautiful meadows to shady woodlands. Along the way, you'll spot all sorts of wildlife, including butterflies and birds.

Gosnold Trails: These winding trails provide stunning views across the island and out to sea. With over 5 miles of paths to explore, there's something for everyone here.

Upland Trail: Take a 3-mile hike through scenic forests and open fields in this unspoiled part of Martha's Vineyard. Keep an eye out for wildflowers and birds while enjoying this peaceful walk.

Long Point Wildlife Refuge Trail: This 2-mile trail takes visitors through wetlands, dunes, and meadows. Be sure to keep an eye out for the wide variety of wildlife here - from snowy owls to foxes and more.

Wenemoyne State Forest: Go for a 4-mile hike at this scenic state forest, located in Chilmark. You'll find plenty of lush trails winding through ancient oak forests and open pastures.

Whether you're looking for a leisurely stroll or an adventurous trek, Martha's Vineyard has plenty of nature walks to enjoy!

Famous Cemeteries

The **Indian Hill Cemetery**, located in West Tisbury, is one of the most historically significant cemeteries on Martha's Vineyard. It is a reminder of the island's Native American heritage and serves as a memorial for those who lived here before European settlers arrived. The cemetery sits along an ancient Wampanoag trail, which gives visitors an insight into how life was lived in the area centuries ago.

The cemetery itself dates back hundreds of years, with some of the gravestones indicating that they were placed there as early as 1690. Many of these markers are inscribed with symbols and images that hold cultural significance to the native tribespeople who once used this area as their hunting grounds.

Many graves in Indian Hill Cemetery belong to members of the Wampanoag tribe, but there are also several graves belonging to English settlers who came to Martha's Vineyard in the late 1700s and early 1800s. These graves are decorated with more traditional Christian symbols such as crosses and cherubs, reflecting their spiritual beliefs.

Within its grounds, Indian Hill Cemetery contains several notable grave sites, such as that of Mary Mayhew, the first female African American school teacher on Martha's Vineyard. Her grave is marked with a plaque honoring her legacy and dedication to educating others about history and culture. Another notable site is that of Peter Bennet Jr., a whaling captain who died during an ill-fated voyage around Cape Horn in 1853; his grave has been honored with a commemorative plaque from his family expressing their love for him and gratitude for his bravery during this journey.

Visiting Indian Hill Cemetery is like taking a step back in time – it offers visitors an opportunity to learn more about Martha's Vineyard's past while paying respects to those who lived here centuries ago. It's no wonder why many people consider it one of the most beautiful cemeteries on Martha's Vineyard – its picturesque grounds provide solace for those seeking peace and reflection amid nature's beauty.

The **Philbin Family Cemetery** in Edgartown is home to headstones that date as far back as 1690. It is believed to be the oldest cemetery in Martha's Vineyard and still serves as a burial ground for members of this historic family who still live on the Island today.

Abel's Hill Cemetery is located in Chilmark and holds the graves of Revolutionary War heroes, fishermen, farmers, tradesmen and others who contributed greatly to Martha's Vineyard during its early years. The cemetery dates back to at least 1819 when it was mentioned in records from St. Elizabeth's Church.

Oak Grove Cemetery in Oak Bluffs was started in 1711 with just nine graves but has since grown into over 500 grave markers ranging from traditional slate stones to more modern memorials. It is also known for being one of the best examples of 19th century garden cemeteries in Massachusetts as well as a historic site which reflects the diversity and history of Martha's Vineyard over three centuries.

These cemeteries serve as historical reminders that preserve not only a person's memory but also an entire community's rich cultural heritage - so keep them on your list when looking for things to do while visiting Martha's Vineyard!

Mysteries and Folklore of Martha's Vineyard

Martha's Vineyard is a mysterious and beautiful island. It has long been known as a vacation destination for many families, but also holds many mysteries that remain unsolved to this day. One such mystery revolves around the island's history with pirates.

It was common knowledge among sailors that Martha's Vineyard was once frequented by pirates and privateers who used the island as a haven to store their stolen goods and hide from authorities. In fact, many old documents still tell tales of pirates stashing their loot on the island, though no one ever reported finding any of it. Other records mention strange lights seen on the island late at night, which some claim were pirate signals or other forms of communication.

The rumors around Martha's Vineyard don't stop there - some even speak of buried treasure located somewhere on the island! One popular tale tells of a Spanish galleon carrying gold that sunk off the shore near Chappaquiddick Island in 1641, although this myth has never been proven true.

Martha's Vineyard is also home to several legends about secret passages and hidden rooms that were supposedly used by pirates and other criminals as hideouts or secret lairs. Some say these areas contained treasure troves filled with precious metals and jewels, while others suggest they may hold clues to long-forgotten mysteries or lost artifacts. The truth behind these stories remains unknown, but whatever secrets are hiding there are sure to be fascinating!

Martha's Vineyard has a long and rich history of folklore. One of the most prominent themes in the folklore of Martha's Vineyard is that of the legendary sea creature, known as the Grandfather Cod. This giant fish has been said to protect fishermen from harsh weather, and it has also been said to bring luck to those who honor it.

The legend of the Grandfather Cod dates to colonial times, when it was first described by settlers as a large fish-like creature resembling an ancient sea serpent. The earliest accounts tell tales about how this benevolent creature would appear in moments of great danger or distress, helping sailors survive turbulent storms and providing guidance on their journeys. Although there is no physical evidence to support this belief, local fishermen continue to report seeing a giant cod swimming alongside their vessels during rough seas.

Another popular folk tale is that of ghost ships. Sailors have reported seeing ghostly vessels sailing around Martha's Vineyard in the night, usually accompanied by eerie lights and spectral music. Depending on which version you hear, these mysterious ships may be crewed by either cursed pirates or lost souls searching for redemption; either way they make for some fascinating stories!

In addition to tales about supernatural creatures, Martha's Vineyard also boasts several other traditional folktales passed down through generations. From humorous stories about trickster creatures such as raccoons and cats, to mysterious tales involving hidden treasure or enchanted forests - all these stories contribute to understanding both the beauty and uniqueness of this special part of New England.

Martha's Vineyard has also been home to unusual rituals and customs over the years, including that of "frailing." This practice involves burning juniper branches over open coals to create smoke which is believed to ward off evil spirits and misfortune. While "frailing" may sound strange today, it was once widely practiced throughout Martha's Vineyard by both Native Americans and early settlers alike!

The folklore and traditions associated with Martha's Vineyard are an important part of its cultural heritage - something all visitors should take time out to explore during their stay on this beautiful island. From mythical creatures like the Grandfather Cod protecting fishermen at sea, spectral ghost ships bringing messages from beyond, right down through to quaint rituals like "frailing," there are plenty of interesting tales awaiting discovery!

Martha's Vineyard's Indigenous People

The Aquinnah Tribe

Whether you're traveling along twisting roads, observing acres of unspoiled landscapes or standing awestruck on the island's iconic red cliffs, the history and culture of the Aquinnah people permeate Martha's Vineyard.

Achieving federal recognition as a distinct tribe of the Wampanoag Nation in 1987, the Aquinnah have inhabited Martha's Vineyard (Noepe in the tribal language) for at least 10,000 years. Once numbering some 3,000 people, the Aquinnah – like Indigenous people across North America – suffered a heavy toll following the arrival of European settlers who brought unfamiliar diseases and battles for control and ownership of the land. Today's Aquinnah tribe comprises about 900 members, approximately 300 of whom live on Martha's Vineyard.

The tribe's ancestral lands in southwestern Martha's Vineyard - including the red clay cliffs - became known as Gay Head following incorporation of the area as a town by white settlers in 1870. The tribe's territory became confined to the region from Nashaquitsa Pond to the cliffs, an area known as an "Indian District."

Concern for further potential encroachment on tribal lands led to formation of the Wampanoag Tribal Council of Gay Head, Inc. in 1972 to preserve native history and culture, work toward federal recognition of the tribe and seek return of tribal lands. The US government eventually granted the tribe some restitution for land unjustly taken. The Massachusetts Legislature officially renamed Gay Head as Aquinnah, its Wampanoag name, in 1998.

Governed by a Tribal Council, the Aquinnah people now steward and oversee 477 acres of ancestral lands. While enriching the overall fabric of island life as active citizens and business owners, the Aquinnah

81

ensure continuation of their own culture by teaching traditional arts such as beadwork and pottery, and through festivals such as Cranberry Day - held the second Tuesday of October to celebrate the harvest of sasumaneash, the sturdy, sour berries Wampanoags relied upon as a winter staple for millennia.

The Aquinnah Cultural Center opened in 2006 with a mission "to preserve, educate and document the Aquinnah Wampanoag self-defined history, culture and contributions past, present and future".

Martha's Vineyard in World War II

Throughout the years of World War II, Martha's Vineyard was an important part of the allied effort. During this time, the island played host to military installations such as a Naval Air Station, Army base, Coast Guard facilities, and many others.

The Naval Air Station on Martha's Vineyard offered training exercises for pilots throughout the war. It serviced both blimps and float planes for anti-submarine warfare as well as helping with search and rescue operations. The Navy also built a very large radio direction finding station at Gay Head that was used to detect hostile aircraft and U-boats approaching from Europe.

The Army had two main bases on Martha's Vineyard - **Camp Edwards** and **Camp Gouge** - which were used to train men entering the service around 1942. The base was home to thousands of soldiers who would often pass through onto troop ships bound for overseas duty. Local residents and businessmen would sometimes take some of these soldiers out fishing or clamming during their stay.

These bases played an important role in defending the coasts against enemy attack and provided a much-needed morale boost for American troops abroad by allowing them to visit family back home while they trained on the island. Later in the war, Martha's Vineyard became a recreation center where veterans could rest and recuperate before being sent back into the fight.

The United States Coast Guard had a large presence during the war years. They were responsible for patrolling off shore areas, rescuing downed pilots, and protecting ships from enemy submarines. The Coast Guard station at Oak Bluffs on Martha's Vineyard saw plenty of action during WWII.

One of the most popular destinations for visiting personnel during World War II was South Beach on Martha's Vineyard. A favorite for leisure and recreation, South Beach saw a surge of activity as thousands passed through looking for relaxation or respite from training and battlefronts.

The beach had a special place in the hearts of many servicemen who were given the rare opportunity to swim in the beautiful waters off-duty. It was also home to clubhouses that offered a variety of activities including movies, dances, and other entertainment. For many young men at war, these activities provided some solace in an otherwise uncertain time.

Civilians also flocked to South Beach, offering food, souvenirs, and all sorts of other goods to visiting personnel. The atmosphere was vibrant and exciting - providing much needed comfort to those who had left family and friends behind.

South Beach is remembered fondly by those who spent time there during World War II as a place of solace where people could come together despite their differences in order to enjoy some peace and camaraderie during this tumultuous time.

Notable Women of Martha's Vineyard

Martha's Vineyard is a unique, popular destination which has a wide range of notable women who have made an impact on the island and beyond. From successful entrepreneurs to long-time residents, these women have contributed in many ways, becoming pillars of strength in the community.

The first woman to make an impact on Martha's Vineyard was **Abigail Mayhew**, a Quaker farmer who moved to the island with her husband in 1671. She quickly became an integral part of the community, providing food and necessities to those in need. She was also a vocal advocate for education, helping to establish the first schoolhouse on the island.

Elizabeth Taber served as selectman of Edgartown from 1803-1807. During this time she championed multiple causes such as improved public infrastructure, education reform and promotion of industry in order to improve the economic conditions of the island.

Emily Howland was an educator, philanthropist and lifelong resident of Martha's Vineyard who established a petition for women's right to vote in 1870. Her efforts were successful, leading to Massachusetts becoming one of the first states to allow women to cast ballots in presidential elections that year.

Margaret Mitchell Freese who was dedicated to preserving Martha's Vineyard historic architecture by founding "Preservation Trust."

Barbara Flanders, who served as the first woman President of the Martha's Vineyard Savings Bank from 1995-2002. During her tenure she championed causes such as affordable housing and community development, helping to transform the economic landscape of the island.

Ellen McCulloch-Lovell, who was appointed by Governor Deval Patrick to serve as Secretary of Education in 2009. She has advocated for high-quality education systems and increased access to higher education on the island, spearheading many initiatives that have helped thousands of students gain access to their dreams and opportunities.

Annie Wananarka has also made great strides in furthering women's rights on the Island, having spearheaded multiple initiatives aimed at empowering women in business and politics. She was a founding board member of Women Working Together (WWT), an organization that focuses on inspiring and advocating for equality through leadership development and capacity building among women.

Julia Child, who called Martha's Vineyard home for many years after she retired from television. Her iconic cookbooks and TV show not only revolutionized French cooking for Americans but also inspired generations of future chefs around the world.

Emma Noyes, who established the first school for African-American children in Oak Bluffs in 1904.

Henrietta Shearer, wife of Charles Shearer was behind the success of the Shearer Cottage by opening a very successful laundry. The money enabled Charles to build and open the famous Shearer Cottage.

Dorothy West (June 2, 1907 – August 16, 1998) was an American storyteller and short story writer during the time of the Harlem Renaissance. She is best known for her 1948 novel *The Living Is Easy*, as well as many other short stories and essays, about the life of an upper-class black family. Documentary filmmaker Salem Mekuria used West as one of the principal sources for her half-hour study of the Black community on Martha's Vineyard, *Our Place in the Sun* (1988), and then created a biographical study *As I Remember It: A Portrait of Dorothy West* (1991). Both received Emmy nominations.

After her re-emergence as a writer, she was a celebrated figure on the Vineyard. Guests at her 90th birthday party included Henry Louis Gates Jr., Anita Hill, Jessye Norman and Charles Ogletree.

Chappaquiddick

It neighbors Martha's Vineyard on the east, and sometimes a slender beach connects it to the rest of the Vineyard along the south. On a map, it looks big, with a great barrier beach hooking wide and long over the top, but the actual landmass is small, only about thirty-eight hundred acres. Chappaquiddick is as much an island of bays and ponds and inlets as it is of hills and fields and forests.

Chappaquiddick was created during the last ice age, shoveled and dumped into place by the same glacier that built up the rest of the Vineyard around 21,000 years ago. In fact the hills of Chappy, the Vineyard, and Nantucket mark the end of the line for the great ice sheet; the glacier would advance no farther to the southeast than these three future Islands, and on retreat, it would leave behind the most recently deposited – and therefore geologically newest – ground in all of New England.

The first settlers, ancestors to the modern Wampanoags, arrived from Asia and the continent well after the ice pulled back into Canada, roughly 12,000 years ago, but still long before the Islands were surrounded by water. The seafloor in this epoch was still a cold, vast, and inhospitable coastal plain, with the waters of the Atlantic Ocean lying hundreds of miles to the south.

But it's worth noting here that Chappaquiddick isn't always an island unto itself. A slender stretch of South Beach known as Norton Point sometimes connects the southern shore of Chappaquiddick to the southern shore of Martha's Vineyard, and in these periods, which can last for decades, Chappy is technically a peninsula of the Vineyard. Yet great storms and tides periodically bust open this beach to the ocean, separating Chappy from the rest of the Vineyard for decades more – which probably accounts for the transitory meaning of the word Chappaquiddick: "at the separated island." Most recently the bay broke through the beach to the ocean during the Patriots' Day Storm of April 2007, and since then Chappy has been an island in fact as well as spirit.

From the start, Chappy was different from the rest of the Vineyard, a wild and buffering outpost of hills but few plains, of rock but mostly thin and sandy soil. Facing north, east, and south, Chappaquiddick shielded much of the eastern half of Martha's Vineyard from coastal storms even as it took the brunt of these gales itself. Set off by itself, a frontier in every way, the island became the home of the hardy Chappaquiddicks, one of four tribes to occupy the Vineyard and its large satellite island. The Chappaquiddicks fished from the shoreline, cleared land by fire, grew crops, whaled from shore, hunted, and quahogged in the verdant shell fishing beds of Cape Pogue Pond.

The first white colonists settled Edgartown, just across the harbor entrance from Chappaquiddick Point, in 1642. Thomas Mayhew Sr., his son Thomas Jr., and a clutch of perhaps thirty other settlers from townships near Boston were looking for an outpost of their own, an island where they could run their own affairs, both politically and in trade. Once established in Edgartown, these newcomers quickly proclaimed Chappaquiddick to be a part of their own village, and from fall to spring pastured their livestock there because they knew they did not need to build fences to keep it from wandering off.

The settlers, it must be said, brought calamity to the Chappaquiddicks, who fell victim to diseases for which they had no biological defenses, whose lands were overrun by livestock, and whose deeply spiritual lives they were called upon to forsake when Thomas Jr. began to teach them about the commandments of a Christian God. The first convert to Christianity in all of New England was in fact a Chappaquiddick native, Hiacoomes, who himself became a revered pastor, not only to his fellow natives but to the English who had introduced him to their own puritan faith.

The first of these new settlers set up homes on Chappy around 1750. With the surviving Chappaquiddicks relegated to less productive ground lying north of what is now the main road on the island, the newcomers fished the waters and farmed the land. To a remarkable and particular degree, they also took up the adventurous life of offshore whaling. In

1871, the Vineyard Gazette listed forty Chappaquiddick men who had risen to the rank of whaling master, possibly the largest number per capita of any place on earth. Among them was Captain William A. Martin (1829-1907), one of the few men of color to achieve the rank.

In the first years of the nineteenth century, Edgartown – which never had a large whaling fleet of its own – established itself as a seaport known for the skill of its whaling masters and the effectiveness of its waterfront industries, especially rigging, ship repair, processing catches, and provisioning whalers for new voyages. Across the harbor, Chappaquiddick evolved into a place of business too.

On the Point in the early 1800s there was a large saltworks, and across the island one could find at least one boatbuilder, and a thriving shellfishery that boats as far away as Connecticut came to buy from. At faraway Wasque Point there were also pilots who braved wild seas, un-forgiving shoals, and merciless currents to row surfboats miles out to schooners and whalers, where the pilots would board the vessels and guide them safely into port.

With the collapse of whaling after the Civil War, Edgartown slid into a depression from which it would take decades to fully recover, a decline that would also transform the village from a place that made its money from industry to one that made it off of leisure. But resorthood was slow to come to the old seaport. Most visitors and summer residents confined themselves to neighboring Cottage City (now Oak Bluffs), a merry town of hotels, promenades, and amusements that grew up sud-denly in the postwar boom, surrounding what today is a tranquil enclave known as the Camp Ground, but which was then a spectacularly large and famous summertime meeting of converts to evangelical Methodism.

Yet Chappy, separated and self-reliant, felt the economic suffering of Edgartown less – mostly because it had never prospered that extrava-gantly to begin with. The ferry between Chappy and its parent town, in business at least since 1807, was nothing more than a rowboat at the end of the nineteenth century, which signifies how little commerce probably was going back and forth between town and island in this period. In the 1870s, there were as yet no summer residents on Chappy, no stores, noth-ing resembling a village. Just a few houses, a few farms, a meetinghouse standing bravely atop the highest, scrubbiest hill, and a one-room schoolhouse for white children and the few Wampanoag youngsters who remained.

If anything snapped Chappy forward into the modern era, it came across the harbor by barge on Thursday, July 18, 1912:

"We understand the first automobile on the island of Chappaquiddick went careering over hill and dale yesterday afternoon," reported the Vineyard Gazette. "It was taken over on a large scow and belongs to Dr. Frank L. Marshall of Boston, who has a summer place near Joel's Landing. We are told the frequent honks as it proceeded to the Doctor's place so aroused some of the staid inhabitants that Gov. Handy" – William Handy, a Chappy deliveryman and jack-of-all trades who rarely left the island – "came to town to see what it was all about."

But the first genuine car-and-passenger ferry – a scow with its own engine and helm, designed by Tony Bettencourt, the ferry owner, and considered revolutionary at the time – did not go into service until the spring of 1935, and by that point, Chappy was as fully ensnared by the seasonal demands of resorthood as the Vineyard as a whole was.

Yes, many Chappaquiddickers still lived principally off the water and the land. But now there was a bathing beach on the Point (now the Chappy Beach Club) filled in July and August with hundreds of visitors from the town, laundry trucks bounced over the dirt roads of Chappy with fresh linens for summer residents, and year-round Chappaquiddickers took on the same jobs in service of summer folks as year-round Edgartonians were on their side of the harbor.

Yet well into the twentieth century, by accident of geography and the quiet determination of residents both all-year and seasonal, Chappy remained just difficult enough to reach that it kept its outback feel. What houses that remained were few and scattered. No business district grew or spread. The one main road remained only partially paved. Forests grew over the old farming fields, but the island held on to its austere beauty – a wild, wind-blasted, tangled, gray-green unkemptness that invited all but the most inquiring and adventurous souls to almost forget that it was even there.

All this changed, of course, on the night of July 18, 1969, when Senator Ted Kennedy drove off a bridge and a young lady died.

Overnight, the accident transformed Chappaquiddick. What had been an island that few beyond New England had ever heard of was now among the most discussed and investigated places on the planet. Like Watergate and its association with political scandal, Chappaquiddick became a byword for tragedy, intrigue, and dynastic upheaval. And for everyone associated with Chappy, whether from birth or by choice, the essential characteristics of the island – its isolation and disassociation from anything larger than itself – was, in a morning, forever lost.

Even so, the Chappaquiddick of today retains a full measure of its rugged outpost spirit and beauty. There is no place on the Vineyard as a whole – and by extension, no place on the globe – that resembles it.

Across the landscape and along the endless shoreline, visitors discover an astounding and diverse array of oceanfront and inland wildlife preserves, the largest owned and managed by The Trustees of Reservations, a state conservation agency, and others, just as memorable, by the Martha's Vineyard Land Bank Commission. There are unmatched opportunities to angle for bluefish and striped bass up and down the ocean and outer harbor beaches. There are walking trails across Chappy that lead to vistas of startling beauty. And there is just one retail business, The Chappy Store ("A Tradition Since 8 am"), which offers a few sundries to seasonal passersby and whose existence strongly suggests that, on Chappy, if the store doesn't carry it, you probably don't need it.

In one crucial, geographical way, Chappaquiddick today remains what it has always been: a destination, in many respects, the final stop. The same sense of adventure that brings residents and visitors to the Vineyard in the first place inspires a certain percentage to go one island further. Chappy is not for everybody. It never has been. But those who really ought to experience it, whether as a resident or a visitor – well, one day, sooner or later, they always will.

The Chappaquiddick Ferry

What Residents of Martha's Vineyard Know But Visitors Do Not

The natives of Martha's Vineyard know much more about the island than visitors do. For one, the island is full of history and culture that only locals are aware of. Many families have been on the island for generations, and their stories provide a depth to the area that can't be found elsewhere.

The native population has also developed a unique form of language known as "Hinglish", which is a combination of English, African-American Vernacular English, and parts of the Wampanoag Language. This language adds another layer to the rich cultural experience that visitors don't get exposed to.

Martha's Vineyard is also home to some amazing wildlife. The waters around the island are teeming with species like humpback whales, endangered Kemp's Ridley sea turtles, gray seals and harbor porpoises. In addition, birds such as black oystercatchers and piping plovers come to nest in certain areas of the island during certain times of year.

For those looking for outdoor activities, Martha's Vineyard offers plenty in terms of hiking trails, beaches, and parks. With over 50 miles of coastline and numerous state forests and conservation areas, there's something for everyone to enjoy here. Whether it's exploring some of Martha's Vineyard's secluded beaches or going on a hike through lush landscapes, visitors can take advantage of all this gorgeous scenery in short order should they choose to stay on the island overnight or longer.

In addition to its natural beauty, Martha's Vineyard also offers an impressive selection of restaurants featuring fresh seafood caught daily from local fishermen along with local produce grown right on the island itself. Visitors won't find better seafood anywhere else! Plus there are plenty of other dining options including family-style eateries with plenty of cozy cafes for coffee lovers who want something unique during their visit—all offering delectable fare made from scratch by culinary masters who know how to capture the flavor profile that makes Martha's Vineyard so special!

So while visitors may be familiar with visiting Martha's Vineyard's top tourist attractions like Edgartown Harbor Lighthouse or Chappaquiddick Beach, there is really so much more than meets the eye when it comes this beautiful place if you just scratch beneath its surface—which is why locals love it so much!

For Birdwatchers – Do You Know?

For lovers of nature, Martha's Vineyard has a wealth of wildlife to observe from its many forests and wildlife reserves. There are plenty of trails to explore if you're feeling up for a hike or bike ride. Birdwatchers will also have plenty to see - there are over 200 species of birds on the island! Many endangered species can also be spotted here including piping plovers and roseate terns.

Four Seasons – Do You Know?

Martha's Vineyard offers something new each season - in fall, take part in the annual Island-wide Festival featuring art shows and music performances; in winter enjoy ice skating on one of the many ponds; while in spring admire the beautiful wildflowers that bloom across the island. Summertime is great for exploring all Martha's Vineyard has to offer - from beaches, lighthouses and quaint towns to abundant wildlife reserves and outdoor activities like hiking and kayaking!

Trivia Section

Trivia Questions

1. Before the establishment of Edgartown in 1642 and the arrival of European explorers, Martha's Vineyard was known as "what" by the native Wampanoag Tribe of Aquinnah/Gay Head?

   A. Martha's Island
   B. Holmes' Hole
   C. Noepe
   D. Aquinnah

2. Which island town was the first village on Martha's Vineyard to have electricity in the home and was the first resort town?

   A. Edgartown
   B. Cottage City
   C. Oak Bluffs
   D. Tisbury

3. For over 150 years, this September Island event signifies the end of the traditional summer season and used to be marked by the annual visit of the Massachusetts Governor to the island.

   A. The Ag Fair
   B. Illumination Night
   C. Tisbury Town Fair
   D. Beach Road Concert Series

4. This church's stained-glass windows were designed and made by Louis C. Tiffany (founder of Tiffany & Co.) in 1899.

   A. The Federated Church
   B. St. Andrew's Church
   C. St. Vincent's Church
   D. The Tabernacle

97

5. This famous comedian is buried at Chilmark Cemetery, South Road.

    A. George Carlin
    B. Robin Williams
    C. Lou Costello
    D. John Belushi

6. Known as "The Mother of Etiquette", this world-famous author, newspaper columnist, radio-host and magazine contributor made Edgartown her summer home from 1927 until her death in 1960.

    A. Emily Dickerson
    B. Emily Post
    C. Ayn Rand
    D. Florence Hartley

7. In 1977, what two states invited Martha's Vineyard to become part of their states during its possible secession from the Commonwealth?

    A. Rhode Island and New Jersey
    B. Connecticut and New York
    C. Maine and New Hampshire
    D. Vermont and Hawaii

8. What animal is featured on the Martha's Vineyard "separatists' flag" when island residents considered becoming the 51st state in the US?

    A. A Great White Shark
    B. A Seagull
    C. A Black Dog
    D. A Blue Lobster

9. Which island restaurant has full strips of bacon at the bar instead of popcorn, peanuts or chex-mix for happy hour from 4pm to 7pm?

    A. The Atlantic
    B. The Wharf
    C. The Ritz
    D. State Road Restaurant

10. Which former First Lady had a summer home on Upper Main Street in Vineyard Haven?

    A. "Lady Bird" Johnson
    B. Jacqueline Kennedy
    C. Hillary Clinton
    D. Michelle Obama

11. How many golf courses are there on the island?

    A. Two
    B. Three
    C. Four
    D. Five

12. Which former President drops signed presidential golf balls on the fairway while he plays to "apologize" for causing delays?

    A. Bill Clinton
    B. George Bush
    C. Barack Obama
    D. Donald Trump

13. How much did the Obamas pay for their secluded 29-acre home in Edgartown, formerly owned by Boston Celtics owner Wycliffe Grousbeck?

    A. Nothing, it was a gift
    B. $11.7 million
    C. $8.6 million
    D. $19.5 million

14. How much did Jacqueline Kennedy Onassis pay for her 340-acre compound in Aquinnah in 1979?

    A. She inherited the land
    B. $20.3 million
    C. $1.1 million
    D. $15.9 million

15. What's the name of the oldest house on Martha's Vineyard?

   A. The Vincent House
   B. Martha's Cabin
   C. The Miller House
   D. Tilton's Cottage

16. What does the island population increase to during the peak of the summer season from its estimated 16,000 year-round population?

   A. Approx. 50,000
   B. Approx. 90,000
   C. Approx. 200,000
   D. Approx. 150,000

17. What is the name of the oldest hotel on Martha's Vineyard?

   A. The Mansion House
   B. The Wesley
   C. The Harbor View
   D. Martha's Bed & Breakfast

18. How many towns are there on the Vineyard?

   A. Four
   B. Five
   C. Six
   D. Two

19. Which town is the youngest town on island?

   A. Menemsha
   B. Vineyard Haven
   C. Chilmark
   D. Oak Bluffs

20. Who was the first President to visit and vacation on Martha's Vineyard?

    A. George Washington
    B. John F. Kennedy
    C. Ulysses S. Grant
    D. Grover Cleveland

21. What is the affectionate nickname given to a year-round resident who was not born on island or who did not grow-up on island?

    A. A Layover
    B. A Wash-a-Shore
    C. A Stowaway
    D. A Hitch-a-Ride

22. How many commercial vineyards or wineries are located on the Vineyard?

    A. 15 commercial vineyards and one winery
    B. 10 winery vineyards and 2 commercial vineyards
    C. None
    D. 6 commercial vineyards and 6 winery vineyards

23. Name the annual fundraising event which signifies the "kick-off" of the island summer season?

    A. The Taste of the Vineyard or "The Taste"
    B. The Annual Beach Clean-up
    C. Noepe Wash-a-Shore Cocktail Party
    D. Showboat

24. Which towns are considered "up-island"?

    A. Edgartown and Oak Bluffs
    B. Vineyard Haven and Chappy
    C. West Tisbury, Chilmark and Aquinnah
    D. Chappy, East Chop and West Chop

25. During the peak summer months, which towns restricts their public beaches to their town residents only?

A. Vineyard Haven, Edgartown and Oak Bluffs
B. West Tisbury and Chilmark
C. Tisbury and Chappaquiddick
D. All the towns

26. Prior to the release of the 1974 movie "Jaws" by Steven Spielberg, what was the approximate number of annual summer vacationers?

A. 10,000
B. 5,000
C. 90,000
D. 35,000

27. What is the percentage of legal island residents who do not have health insurance?

A. 0%
B. 70%
C. 50%
D. 43%

28. How many lighthouses does the island of Martha's Vineyard have?

A. Three
B. Six
C. Two
D. Five

29. Due to climate change and beach erosion, which island lighthouse had to be moved 150 feet to avoid possibly falling into the ocean in 2015?

A. Gay Head
B. Cape Pogue
C. West Chop
D. Edgartown

30. Which town has the only statue north of the Mason-Dixon Line to honor Confederate Soldiers of the Civil War?

    A. Edgartown
    B. Tisbury
    C. Chilmark
    D. Oak Bluffs

31. What was the name of the first Jewish settlers to make a permanent home on Martha's Vineyard?

    A. The Halls
    B. The Brickmans
    C. The Cronigs
    D. The Levinsons

32. In the movie "Jaws," which ferry does Richard Dreyfus' character, Hooper appear on when he is arriving to the island of Amity?

    A. The Piped Piper
    B. The Chappy Ferry
    C. The Island Queen
    D. The Patriot

33. What major computer software company founder has a fabulous Victorian mansion on the perimeter of Ocean Park in Oak Bluffs?

    A. Peter Norton
    B. Bill Gates
    C. Elon Musk
    D. Steve Jobs

34. Which famous "Cheers" cast member owns a home in Chilmark?

    A. Woody Harrelson
    B. Ted Danson
    C. Kirstie Alley
    D. Kelsey Grammer

35. Which famous film director lives near the 14th fairway on Farm Neck Golf Course during the summer?

    A. Steve Spielberg
    B. Guy Richie
    C. Spike Lee
    D. Martin Scorsese

36. Which public beach is known for gathering crowds every sunset because the sun seems to melt into the water?

    A. Lamberts Cove
    B. Long Point
    C. South Beach
    D. Menemsha Beach

37. Which island restaurant has an incognito cocktail lounge tucked away upstairs that resembles a private study?

    A. Nancy's
    B. Alchemy
    C. The Atlantic
    D. Beetlebung's

38. Which competitive event is held at the Annual Ag Fair that only allows women to participate?

    A. Knitting
    B. The Iron Skillet Toss
    C. Pie Eating Contest
    D. Tractor Pull

39. Which author is known for his Martha's Vineyard Mystery novels?

    A. Phillip Craig
    B. Herman Melville
    C. James Patterson
    D. Tom Clancy

40. How many traffic lights are there on Martha's Vineyard?

    A. One
    B. Ten
    C. Twelve
    D. Four

41. What is the structure called which is in the middle of the 7-acre Ocean Park?

    A. The Gazebo
    B. The Bandstand
    C. The Hut
    D. The Ocean Shack

42. What are the structures, often a glass room, on the top of a house on the Vineyard called?

    A. The Penalty Box
    B. The Quiet Room
    C. A Widow's Perch
    D. The Attic

43. What famous kidnapping is associated with Martha's Vineyard?

    A. The Lindberg Kidnapping
    B. The Patty Hearst Kidnapping
    C. The Frank Sinatra Jr. Kidnapping
    D. The Adam Walsh Kidnapping

44. Which carnivore predators and/or poisonous reptiles live on Martha's Vineyard?

    A. Bobcat, Black Bears and Rattlesnakes
    B. Redtail Hawks, Bald Eagles, Turkey Vultures and Ospreys
    C. Mountain Lions, Coral Snakes and Copperheads
    D. Grizzly Bears, Wolves, Foxes, and poisonous lizards

45. Which author did Jacqueline Kennedy Onassis serve as editor for, whom Jackie would visit on island to edit and proofread the author's second novel, *The Wedding*, which was dedicated to Jackie O?

    A. Dorothy West
    B. Cynthia Riggs
    C. Rose Styron
    D. Melinda Fagen

46. What famous politician's house is located two doors away from Dorothy West's home in Oak Bluffs?

    A. Barack Obama
    B. Bill Clinton
    C. Adam Clayton Powell
    D. Frank Lautenberg

47. What is the name of the beach located in the middle of the town in Oak Bluffs?

    A. The Bend in the Road Beach
    B. Fuller Beach
    C. The Inkwell
    D. East Chop Beach

48. Which lighthouse is also called Telegraph Hill?

    A. Gay Head Lighthouse
    B. East Chop Lighthouse
    C. West Chop Lighthouse
    D. Edgartown Lighthouse

49. Why was the Martha's Vineyard Airport originally established?

    A. To bring more visitors to the island
    B. To improve access of goods and services to the island
    C. It served as a training facility, so pilots could practice landing on aircraft carriers
    D. To provide alternative evacuation option for islanders

50. Which famous actress from the 1990's has a vacation home on Chappaquiddick?

    A. Halle Berry
    B. Kim Bassinger
    C. Meg Ryan
    D. Julia Roberts

51. When traveling from up-island, Vineyard Haven or Oak Bluffs into downtown Edgartown, which road should one take to avoid the bottleneck at the triangle on Vineyard Haven Road?

    A. Pease Point Way
    B. Look Street
    C. Beach Road
    D. Edgartown/West Tisbury Road

52. Which beaches are "clothing optional"?

    A. South Beach and Bend in the Road Beach
    B. Lucy Vincent Beach, Aquinnah/Moshup Beach and Lambert's Cove
    C. East Chop Beach and West Chop Beach
    D. State Beach and Fuller Beach

53. What is the signature drink at Nancy's Restaurant in Oak Bluffs?

    A. The MV Wave
    B. The OB Tide
    C. The Dirty Banana
    D. Anchors Away

54. Where can you see Shakespeare performed live on stage during the summer?

    A. The Performing Arts Center
    B. Live Outdoors at the Tisbury Amphitheater
    C. Owen Park
    D. The Katherine Cornell Theatre

55. Which towns have the most shops and restaurants within walking distance?

    A. Downtown Edgartown and Oak Bluff
    B. Menemsha and Aquinnah
    C. Chilmark and Vineyard Haven
    D. West Tisbury and Chappy

56. What shelled fish is Martha's Vineyard known for?

    A. Lobster
    B. Shrimp
    C. Mussels
    D. Scallops, Oysters, Quahog and Clams

57. How did the Flying Horses, the oldest operating carousel in the country, find its way to staying permanently on Martha's Vineyard?

    A. PT Barnum left it by mistake
    B. It was built here
    C. It was lost in a card game in 1884
    D. A shipwreck off the coast

58. Why was the main strip/street in Oak Bluffs named Circuit Avenue?

    A. Because the town's electricity started on this street
    B. There was a blackout on the island which started on this street
    C. Because they didn't want to have a Main Street
    D. The Methodist Church started having revival meetings on island which led to the establishment of the town between 1863 to 1872 and the name pays homage to "the preacher's circuit".

59. Which famous actress purchased a vacation home in Aquinnah in the summer of 2022?

    A. Lady Gaga
    B. Sandra Bullock
    C. Madonna
    D. Barbra Streisand

60. Which actor made the newspapers in August 2018 for pouring a drink on Peter Simon, singer Carly Simon's brother, after an altercation?

    A. Dan Akroyd
    B. Dwayne "The Rock" Johnson
    C. Tom Cruise
    D. Bill Murray

61. Which gym did former President Obama use on island before he became President and before he was even a US Senator?

    A. The Mansion House Gym
    B. B-Strong Fitness
    C. The YMCA
    D. Airport Fitness

62. Which town has the most concentrated number of art galleries within walking distances of each other?

    A. Downtown Edgartown
    B. Vineyard Haven
    C. Oak Bluffs
    D. Chilmark

63. What was the only other fast-food franchise restaurant, beside the local Dairy Queen, to ever be established on Martha's Vineyard?

    A. McDonald's
    B. Burger King
    C. Pizza Hut
    D. Subway

64. Whaling captains lived in Edgartown during the 17th/18th century. Which captain sailed on The Acushnet in 1841 with author Herman Melville?

    A. Captain Valentine Pease
    B. Captain Charles Morgan
    C. Captain Thomas Adam Norton
    D. Captain Tristram Pease Ripley

65. What is the type of tree located at 9 S. Water Street, brought to the island as a seedling in the 1800's? It was later planted about 1833.

    A. Scrub Oak
    B. Japanese Maple
    C. Dogwood
    D. The Pagoda Tree

66. What do the four numbers over the front door of most homes in downtown Edgartown represent?

    A. They represent the house location on the world map
    B. It represents the year the home was originally built
    C. It's the distance the home is from the center of town
    D. It's the winning lottery numbers the owner won to purchase the home

67. What was the red clay sand from the Gay Head Cliffs used for?

    A. It is believed to provide hygienical benefits for the skin
    B. It was used to make bricks for buildings
    C. It was used to keep critters out one's garden
    D. It had no purpose other except as the origin of Wampanoag Tribe fables

68. Where is the highest elevation on Martha's Vineyard?

    A. The Aquinnah Cliffs
    B. Peaked Hill
    C. Menemsha Hills
    D. Caroline Tuthill Sanctuary

69. Why are the chimneys on the homes around South and North Water Street in Edgartown, painted black around the top?

    A. To hide the soot from showing on the chimney's top
    B. It's a primer coat of paint
    C. It indicated the homeowner's support for the British troops, in the case English forces began to shell/bomb the homes on the coast. It would deter the opposition from targeting those homes
    D. No reason at all

70. Which are the most picturesque roads to take an afternoon or morning drive?

    A. Main Street, Vineyard Haven, and Chase Road
    B. Water Street in Vineyard Haven
    C. Middle Road, North Road, and South Road
    D. West Tisbury Road to Barnes Road

71. Where to get the best Lobster Roll for your money?

    A. The Atlantic
    B. Beach Road Restaurant
    C. Alchemy
    D. Grace Church in Vineyard Haven on Fridays

72. How many hiking trails does Sheriff's Meadow Foundation provide the public on Martha's Vineyard?

    A. Ten
    B. Twenty-two
    C. Fifteen
    D. Eighteen

73. Under what circumstances should someone consider renting or using a moped to get around the island?

    A. If the lines for the bus appear to be too long
    B. If you want to enjoy zipping around the island on your own and let your inner "biker" out
    C. If you are stranded somewhere in a remote part of the island and it's your only ride
    D. Never, ever, ever, ever rent or use a moped on the Vineyard

74. Where is the ideal place to take the kids rain or shine?

    A. Ryan's Family Amusement in Oak Bluffs
    B. The Barn Bowling Alley in Oak Bluffs
    C. The Cove – Miniature Golf and Grill in Tisbury
    D. All these above

75. Where can I get an alcoholic beverage without having to order food?

    A. Edgartown and Oak Bluffs
    B. Chilmark
    C. Aquinnah
    D. West Tisbury

76. Who was the first and only African American to represent Massachusetts in the United States Senate and has a summer home on Nashawena Avenue in Oak Bluffs?

    A. Deval Patrick
    B. Royal Bolling
    C. Ayanna Presley
    D. Edward Brooke III

77. What are the names of the two tall schooner ships that The Black Dog owns and operates for sunset cruises from Vineyard Haven?

    A. The Orca and The Quint
    B. The Santa Maria and The Nina
    C. The Shenandoah and The Alabama
    D. Solitude and Peace of Mind

78. Who was the only skipper for the schooner Shenandoah that sailed out of Vineyard Haven for 62 years?

    A. John Garvey
    B. Patrick Murphy
    C. Robert Douglas
    D. Cecil Farnsworth

79. What was the name of this captain's last schooner tall ship?

    A. The Andrea Gail
    B. The Alice S. Wentworth
    C. The Orca
    D. The Sea Breeze

80. Best sushi on island with a stellar view?

    A. The Lookout Tavern
    B. Nancy's Restaurant
    C. The Atlantic
    D. All the above

81. Which towns have a doggy park?

    A. Oak Bluff and Vineyard Haven
    B. Edgartown and Chilmark
    C. Aquinnah and Menemsha
    D. None of the above

82. Why does the front of the Federated Church in Edgartown face directly towards the neighboring house?

    A. Buildings in the 1800's always faced away from the street
    B. The front of the church was changed because of a hurricane
    C. The church was built prior to the neighboring homes
    D. The church was moved from a different location

83. What is the name of the horticulturist who created an arboretum (an elaborate garden) in the 1670's in West Tisbury to bring unique and rare vegetation to the island?

    A. Martha Stewart
    B. Polly Hill
    C. Rachel Ray
    D. Lizzie Borden

84. What Oak Bluffs venue served as the island's only roller rink in the late 1800's and now serves as a live music venue and pool hall?

    A. The Ritz
    B. The Sand Bar
    C. The Loft
    D. Noman's

85. Which island business below is not an island farm that offers fresh island-grown fruits, vegetables, eggs and/or meat to the public?

    A. Morning Glory Farm in Edgartown
    B. The Allen Farm in Chilmark
    C. Island Alpaca Company
    D. Ghost Island Farm in Vineyard Haven
    E. Mermaid Farm & Dairy 8 Middle Road in Chilmark

86. What is the cheapest cab company on island?

    A. Adam Cab   (All-island service 24hrs)
    B. Your Taxi   (All-island service 24hrs)
    C. Atlantic Cab (All-island service 24hrs)
    D. Uber

87. Which business name is NOT an up-island deli that I "must try before I die" and grab a quick bite to go?

    A. 7A Deli on State Road in West Tisbury
    B. Black Sheep Mercantile by the airport
    C. Menemsha Deli in Menemsha (Chilmark)
    D. Chilmark General Store on South Road
    E. R & B Eatery in Edgartown

88. How much did Rev. Thomas Mayhew pay for Martha's Vineyard, Nantucket, and the Elizabeth Island in 1641 when he purchased them from the Duke of York, leading to establishment of Edgartown in 1642?

    A. 200 pieces of silver
    B. 1,000 gold pieces
    C. Two pieces of driftwood
    D. 10,000 shillings

89. Tony's Market in Oak Bluffs and Fat Ronnie's on Circuit Avenue has the best French fries and onion rings on the island.

   A. True
   B. False

90. Which of the following beaches is NOT accessible by the island's public transportation system - Vineyard Transit Association (VTA)?

   A. South Beach in Katama (Edgartown)
   B. Joseph Silva State Beach in Oak Bluffs and Edgartown
   C. Long Point Beach in West Tisbury
   D. Fuller Beach on Fuller Street in Edgartown
   E. Lucy Vincent Beach

91. All these locations offer public restrooms in each town except for?

   A. The Stop n' Shop parking lot on Water Street in Vineyard Haven
   B. The Visitors Center on Church Street in Edgartown
   C. The building next to Steamship Authority Terminal in Oak Bluffs
   D. The building across the street from Larsen's Fish Market in Menemsha
   E. Cannonball Park in Edgartown
   F. The Chilmark Library at Beetlebung Corner in Chilmark
   G. The foot of hill at The Gay Head Cliffs in Aquinnah
   H. The West Tisbury Library across for Alley's General Store

92. This university professor and PBS program host gained notoriety when he locked himself out of his Cambridge house and ended up in a dispute with a local police officer. After meeting with the officer at The White House for "the beer summit," he can be seen daily in the summer months riding his three-wheeled bicycle on State Beach in Oak Bluffs. If you see him, just yell, "hey Skippy" to hear the bright chimes of his bell on his bike, as he responds back. His name is?

   A. Charles Ogletree
   B. Dr. Henry Louis Gates
   C. Robert Smith
   D. Jonathan Capehart

93. Which of the following are the names of the only two micro-breweries on Martha's Vineyard?

    A. Hook, Line and Sinker Brewery in Aquinnah
    B. Offshore Ale Brew Pub on Kennebec Avenue in Oak Bluffs
    C. Harp Micro-brew in West Tisbury
    D. Mad Martha's Farmers Brewery on Upper Main Street in Edgartown

94. A bike is a great way to travel the Island?

    A. True
    B. False

95. The name Martha was the explorer Bartholomew Gosnold's daughter's name and he visited the island in 1602. Naming the island after her explains the "Martha's" element of the renaming. But the "Vineyard" portion of the renaming comes from?

    A. All the vineyards on the island
    B. The large vineyard started by Gosnold the year after his wife Martha died
    C. Early Visitors to the island mistook the multiple beach plum bushes for grapes on the vine or bush
    D. There used to be grape vineyards throughout the island before a brutal winter killed them all

96. What is the name of the outdoor bakery venue with a gigantic stone oven that holds pizza-night every Thursday 5:00 pm to 8:00 pm? You select your topping and watch your pie cook right in front of you.

    A. Stone Cold Bakery
    B. The Orange Peel Bakery
    C. Rock-kee and a Bull winkles in Aquinnah
    D. Wampanoag Treats and Eats

97. All of the listed coffee shops offer the best choices for "java" in their town except?

   A. Mocha Mots Coffee Shop on Circuit Avenue in Oak Bluffs and Main Street, Vineyard Haven
   B. Espresso Love at 17 Church Street, Edgartown
   C. Coffee Obsession at 38 S. Water Street, Edgartown
   D. The Depot Market at 141 Main Street, Edgartown

98. Which establishments below do you visit when you are looking for that great-tasting, old-fashioned diner experience for breakfast or lunch?

   A. The Edgartown Diner located behind the Dukes County Courthouse in Edgartown
   B. The Art Cliff Diner Beach Road in Vineyard Haven
   C. Linda Jean's on Circuit Avenue in Oak Bluffs
   D. The Black Dog Restaurant at 20 Beach Road Extension in VH (not the bakery)
   E. The Plane View Diner at the Martha's Vineyard Airport in West Tisbury
   F. The Waterside Market on Main Street in Vineyard Haven
   G. Among the Flowers at 17 Mayhew Lane, downtown Edgartown
   H. All of the above

99. Let's get serious. Who has the best desserts on island?

   A. The Dairy Queen
   B. The Black Dog's Deep Forest Chocolate Cake and the Carrot Cake
   C. Pie Chicks on Martha's Vineyard's pies in Vineyard Haven
   D. Sweet Bite in Vineyard Haven across from Cumberland Farms
   E. The Scottish Bakehouse gluten-free deserts

100. What is the name of the bakery that opens during the summer season 9:00 pm to 11:30 pm in Oak Bluffs to huge lines of customers?

    A. Backdoor Donuts
    B. Chelsea's Late-night Bakery
    C. Fishbones
    D. Biscuits

101. Which if the following restaurants is NOT a hidden gem for dinner when you want to impress?

    A. The Little House Café and Bakery at 339 State Rd, Vineyard Haven
    B. Lucky Hanks at 218 Upper Main Street, Edgartown
    C. The Sweet Life Cafe' at 63 Circuit Avenue, Oak Bluffs
    D. De'tente Restaurant at 15 Winter Street (Nevin Square), Edgartown
    E. State Road Restaurant at 688 State Road, West Tisbury
    F. The Chilmark Tavern at 9 State Road, Chilmark
    G. Atria Restaurant at 137 Main Street, Edgartown
    H. Sharky's Cantina on Circuit Avenue, Oak Bluffs

102. Where did the name Edgartown originate from?

    A. Rev. Thomas Mayhew wanted to gain favor of the Duke of York, so he named the town after
    B. The Duke of York's son Edgar
    C. Edgar was the name of a mythical giant from Wampanoag folk lore
    D. Edgar was Martha's brother
    E. They misplaced Edward

All businesses referenced in this trivia questionnaire have their own websites for additional information.

Trivia Answers

1. **Answer**: **C. Noepe** - According to local Wampanoag Tribe of Aquinnah/Gay Head historians, the island was known as Noepe or Capawok.

2. **Answer**: **C. Oak Bluff** - Originally part of Edgartown, Oak Bluffs became the first resort town on Martha's Vineyard during its heyday between 1865 and 1873.

3. **Answer**: **B. Illumination Night** - Celebrated every third Wednesday in September, Illumination Night takes place in Oak Bluffs at the Tabernacle with all the surrounding cottages hanging Japanese and Chinese lanterns on their porches.

4. **Answer**: **B. St. Andrews Church** - Located at 34 N. Summer Street in Edgartown, this church leaves its doors open daily from 10:00 am to 4:00 pm to allow people to get close looks at these beautiful windows. BTW- Tiffany signed the stained-glass window on the right-hand side of the altar.

5. **Answer**: **D. John Belushi** - The first-generation Albanian and famous SNL actor would vacation on Martha's Vineyard and had requested to be buried here prior to his sudden death.

6. **Answer**: **B. Emily Post** - Still beautifying the colonial-style town, Emily Post's house at 34 Fuller Street remains a hidden gem for neighbors and visitors. It remains a symbol of the island that Post described as, "the haven of delectable tranquility that all my life I have been searching for..."

7. **Answer: D. Vermont and Hawaii** - Upset over losing their guaranteed seat in the Massachusetts General House of Representatives, residents of Martha's Vineyard considered the possibility of secession from the Commonwealth and also considered becoming the nation's 51st state, which included a state flag.

8. **Answer: B. A Seagull** - A white seagull over an orange disk on a sky-blue background was the flag design chosen and can still be seen flying throughout the island today.

9. **Answer: A. The Atlantic** - A favorite stop for celebrities, locals and visitors, The Atlantic is located at the end of Main Street in Edgartown. Its casual upscale presentation is highlighted by free bacon resting in containers on the bar.

10. **Answer: A. "Lady Bird" Johnson** - Lady Bird Johnson, the gracious widow of former President Lyndon Baines Johnson, had been a summer visitor to the Vineyard for more than 20 years until her death. She rented the Upper Main Street, Vineyard Haven home owned by Charles Guggenheim for a number of those years.

11. **Answer: D. Five** - Two public courses: Mink Meadows Golf Course and Chappaquiddick Golf Course – 9 holes, two private courses: Edgartown Golf Couse and Vineyard Golf Course – 18 holes, and one semi-private: Farm Neck Golf Course – 18 holes.

12. **Answer: C. Barack Obama** - A mainstay at Farm Neck Golf Course and Vineyard Golf in August, the former President is known for purposely leaving signed presidential golf balls on the course during his rounds as a goodwill gesture for any inconvenience his presence may have caused. He also leaves his signed player's card in the golf cart for the next player to find.

13. **Answer: B. $11.7 Million** - In December 2019, the Obamas purchased the sprawling 6,892-square-foot house which sits on 29.3 acres on the Edgartown Great Pond between Slough Cove and Turkeyland Cove, with views of a barrier beach and the ocean. Built in 2001, the home features seven bedrooms, eight and a half baths and several stone fireplaces. There is a two-car garage, a detached barn, a pool and of course a basketball court.

14. **Answer: C. $1.1 million** - Rumored to have been purchased with a portion of the $25 million Jackie O' received from the settlement from Aristotle Onassis's death, which Ted Kennedy negotiated. Red Gate Farm was completed in 1981 and is located on Moshup Trail in Aquinnah. Its entrance is distinguished by what else? A red gate. You can't miss it. And yes, Caroline and her family still vacation there.

15. **Answer: A. The Vincent House** - Built in the 1670's and occupied by descendants for over 250 years, it's located behind The Whaling Church in Edgartown and open daily to the public.

16. **Answer: D. Approx. 150,000** - It's estimated that during the July 4th peak the population increases to this enormous number.

17. **Answer: A. The Mansion House** - Originally named The Tisbury Inn, The Mansion House dates back to 1794.

18. **Answer: C. Six** Edgartown, Oak Bluffs, Tisbury, Chilmark, West Tisbury, and Aquinnah.

19. **Answer: D. Oak Bluffs** - Originally part of Edgartown and later called Cottage City, Oak Bluffs is the youngest town on MV.

20. **Answer: C. Ulysses S. Grant** - In 1874, President Grant was pictured enjoying the "Gingerbread Cottages" and Illumination Night with his family prior to the annual fireworks at Ocean Park on the third Friday in September.

21. **Answer**: **B. A Wash-a-Shore** - It explains itself.

22. **Answer**: **C. NONE** - Martha's Vineyard has had exactly one wine-producing vineyard, which closed in 2008 after 37 years of production. In May, wine-lovers flock to the MV Wine Fest, a multi-day celebration of food and wine and every October the island welcomes the *Martha's Vineyard Food & Wine Festival* for four days and four nights of island fun.

23. **Answer**: **A. Taste of the Vineyard or "The Taste"** - The celebratory Gourmet Stroll is the season's kick-off event, the first of the two-night Taste of the Vineyard affair; guests eat, drink, and dance the night away with new and old friends featuring the island's finest restaurants, caterers, and beverage purveyors.

24. **Answer**: **C. West Tisbury, Chilmark and Aquinnah** - These towns are referred to as "up-island", because as you drive to these towns you will begin to ascend in elevation.

25. **Answer**: **B. West Tisbury and Chilmark** - Lambert's Cove Beach, Squibnocket and Lucy Vincent Beach are open to the public before Memorial Day and after Labor Day, but require a town issued sticker during the summer.

26. **Answer: B. 5,000** - Prior to "the first summer blockbuster," *Jaws*, The Vineyard was relatively a well-kept secret. I guess we see what happens when you get a "bigger boat."

27. **Answer: A. 0%** - Massachusetts offers free health insurance to all who cannot afford it, while also offering residents a state sponsored health insurance public option.

28. **Answer: D. Five** - West Chop, East Chop, Edgartown, Gay Head, and Cape Pogue. The Edgartown, The East Chop and Aquinnah lighthouses allow visitors to go inside and to the top of the lighthouses. Please check the schedule.

29. **Answer: A. Gay Head** - Documented by the PBS program *Nova*, the 2016 episode *"Operation Lighthouse Rescue"* depicts how the Gay Head Lighthouse in Aquinnah had to be moved fully intact to save it from collapsing into the Vineyard Sound. They used logs to roll the entire lighthouse. The program is available to view on PBS.org or YouTube.

30. **Answer: D. Oak Bluffs** - In the 1800's, the Oak Bluffs statue was erected by Charles Strahan, a former Confederate lieutenant who was wounded in battle, moved to the island after the war, and bought a newspaper he renamed the Martha's Vineyard Herald. The statue stands in its original spot next to Ocean Park in front of the Oak Bluffs Police Station.

31. **Answer: C. The Cronigs** - In 1905, Samuel Krengle, who later changed his last name to Cronig arrived on Martha's Vineyard and established Cronig's Market with his brother in 1917. To this day, Cronig's Market is one of two grocery-chains on the island. The other is Stop n' Shop, along with two other independent grocery stores. The Brickmans were the first Jewish couple to be married on the island and established their family's Main Street clothing store in Vineyard Haven, Brickman's, in 1903. It is the oldest store in Tisbury.

32. **Answer: B. The Chappy Ferry** - During the filming of the movie *Jaws*, various island locations were utilized with Edgartown and Menemsha serving as the primary backdrops. We see Richard Dreyfus arrive to the island on the Chappy Ferry, as it comes into the dock of downtown E-town.

33. **Answer: A. Peter Norton** - The green distinguishing Victorian mansion with a red roof was renovated by *This Old House* personality Bob Villa before and after it was burned down to its shell in the early 2000's. Peter Norton is the founder of Norton Antivirus.

34. **Answer: B. Ted Danson** - The actor can be seen around island during the summer months at just about every ice cream shop.

35. **Answer: C. Spike Lee** - This two-house compound uniquely stands out in its luxurious, private surroundings because of the New York Yankees' Flag, which flies well above the tree line for all of Red Sox nation to bear. The flag can be seen as far as a mile away from State Beach.

36. **Answer: D. Menemsha Beach** - Accessible by public transportation and a five minute walk to two of the best fish markets on island. Get there early, get some mussels, steamers from Larson's and bring a bottle of wine.

37. **Answer: B. Alchemy** - Located next to the Dukes County Courthouse, this hidden gem is ideal for a nightcap "closing" or an intimate evening starter. No reservations needed for the lounge.

38. **Answer: B. The Iron Skillet Toss** - One of the premier events for local bragging rights for the next 12 months, a tradition that dates back centuries. And yes, the winner makes the front page of the two local newspapers.

39. **Answer: A. Phillip Craig** - After attending Boston University in 1951, he fell for the Vineyard. He wrote his first novel in 1969 and his last in 2006.

40. **Answer: D. Four** - The four traffic lights are all located at the one drawbridge in Tisbury; two on each side of the bridge and one on each side of the street.

41. **Answer: B. The Bandstand** - Located towards the entrance of the park which hosts the annual end of summer fireworks and Sunday evening concert during the season, The Bandstand was built in the 1800's.

42. **Answer: C. A Widow's Perch** - Often designed to allow the wife of a lost sailor to gaze out upon the ocean, waiting for their loved ones' return.

43. **Answer: A. The Lindberg Kidnapping** - Called the 'crime of the century.' After a $50,000 ransom was paid, the kidnappers gave instructions to look for the child on a boat named Nellie, off the coast of the Vineyard. It was later reported that some ransom money was found on island. The Lindberg couple later retired on MV, where Mrs. Lindberg wrote several books at their home off of North Road in Chilmark.

44. **Answer: B. Redtail Hawks, Bald Eagles, Turkey Vultures and Ospreys** - Because of its location the only dangerous carnivores on the island are in the air. There are no poisonous snakes, reptiles, bears or big cats. But, a few coyotes have washed up on shore attempting to swim to the island.

45. **Answer: A. Dorothy West** - With her small porch serving as their meeting place, Jackie O' would visit Ms. West at her petit home in Oak Bluffs located off Dorothy West Avenue. A friendship founded on the love for literature.

46. **Answer: C. Adam Clayton Powell** - Painted red with white trim Former Congressman Adam Clayton Powell's summer home sits on Dorothy West Avenue with a large plaque noting its relevance.

47. **Answer: C. The Inkwell** - Noted as the first and only beach that people of color could use for centuries prior to desegregation, The Inkwell is located at the foot of Waban Park in OB.

48. **Answer: B. East Chop Lighthouse** - Located in Oak Bluffs on East Chop, The East Chop Lighthouse was also known as Telegraph Hill as it served as the location of the only telegraph on island.

49. **Answer: C. It served as a training facility for pilots learning to land on aircraft carriers** - The island beaches and Noman's island were also used for bombing practice. Live munitions are still being unearthed to this day on local beaches.

50. **Answer: C. Meg Ryan** -A daily visitor to the local bike shop in Edgartown, Meg Ryan can be seen walking around downtown E-town and having dinner or lunch at The Atlantic.

51. **Answer: D. Edgartown/West Tisbury Road** -Every islander knows to avoid Edgartown/Vineyard Haven Road or Beach Road when traveling into Edgartown from outside of town. There are only three roads which go into E-town and the two previously mentioned roads converge together at "the triangle". This causes traffic standstills of up to a mile and half with 20 to 30 minute delays. Travel Barnes Road to West Tisbury Road or State Road to Old County Road to avoid this delay.

52. **Answer: B. Lucy Vincent Beach, Aquinnah/Moshup Beach and Lambert's Cove** - Though the designated areas tend to be in isolation and located on the far ends of the beaches, it is important to be aware when traveling with family.

53. **Answer: C. The Dirty Banana (Nancy's signature mudslide with a banana)**

54. **Answer: B. Live Outdoors at the Tisbury Amphitheater** - Starting in June, the Martha's Vineyard Playhouse presents various Shakespeare plays at The Tisbury Amphitheater. The performances usually start around 6:00 pm.

55. **Answer: A. Downtown Edgartown and Oak Bluff** - Both towns offer shops, restaurants, bars, art galleries, and grocery stores within walking distance of the local hotels.

56. **Answer: D. Scallops, Quahog and Clams** - Seafood is caught daily on the Vineyard, but the really fresh shellfish is served daily at Menemsha Beach at The Menemsha Fish Market or Lawson's Fish Market. Fresh off the boat with hot Lobster Rolls and full Clam Bakes.

57. **Answer: C. It was lost in a card game in 1884** - Built in 1876 in Coney Island, NY and came to the island as part of a traveling circus/fair and was lost by the owner in a late-night card game.

58. **Answer: D. It was named to pay homage to "the preacher's circuit."**

59. **Answer: B. Sandra Bullock** - Ms. Bullock owns at least 17 properties throughout the United States and recently purchased a new investment property in Aquinnah near Squibnocket Beach.

60. **Answer: D. Bill Murray** - The altercation took place at Lola's Restaurant, now called Noman's on Beach Road in Oak Bluffs. Peter was a local photographer with a gallery still on Main Street Vineyard Haven and he took a picture of Bill without *The Caddyshack* actor's permission. Charges were not filed.

61. **Answer: B. B-Strong** - Michelle likes to go to Airport Fitness, but before reaching the top office in the land, Barack would workout at B-Strong Fitness on Kennebec Avenue in the heart of OB. His picture with the owner of the gym hangs in the window facing the street.

62. **Answer: A. Downtown Edgartown** - in the downtown area of Edgartown there are 11 art galleries all within a 7-minute walk of one another.

63. **Answer: D. Subway** - Despite enormous efforts from the big burger franchise, only Subway was able to wash-a-shore briefly in 1996 on Circuit Avenue in Oak Bluffs. Only to yield to the ebb

tide after a year. We've got Fat Ronnie's Burgers on Circuit Avenue.

64. **Answer: A. Captain Valentine Pease** - Captain Pease is reputed to have been the inspiration for Captain Ahab in Melville's Moby Dick. Pease's home is located at 80 S. Water Street and was the former home for actress Patricia Neal.

65. **Answer: D. The Pagoda Tree** - Commonly called *The Flam Tree* in China, this tree is the oldest of its kind on the North America continent and it shades Captain Milton's home built in 1840.

66. **Answer: B. It represents the year the home was originally built** - Since Edgartown is a National Historic Whaling Town, the numbers indicate when the home was originally built. To display the "built date," a specific portion of the original building must still be incorporated in the structure.

67. **Answer: B. It was used to make bricks for building** - These bricks were used to build the original Gay Head Lighthouse and other structures on island.

68. **Answer: B. Peaked Hill** - The highest rise is still being debated; scientist say Peaked Hill is the island's summit. The highest point of 311 feet above sea level. Its cousin, Menemsha Hills, located almost a quarter of a mile away, is renowned on the island as a World War II military lookout and garrison and is 308 feet above sea level. Both are accessible via hiking trails with gorgeous views of the whole island.

69. **Answer: C.** It indicated the homeowner's support for the British troops, in the case English forces began to shell/bomb the homes on the coast. It would deter the opposition from targeting those homes. - Remember the whaling captains were working for the nobles in England and the Royal family.

70. **Answer: C. Middle Road, North Road, and South Road** - All of these roads start in West Tisbury and continue into Chilmark with South Road continuing all the way to the Aquinnah cliffs via State Road. Martha's Vineyard is a rural island with several functioning farms. So, if you like breath-taking scenery with dry-stone walls and gorgeous ocean views, take Music Street to Middle Road in West Tisbury. Then prepared to be transported to the hills of Scotland as you cruise through rolling lush hills framed in century old dry-stone walls that encircle an array of livestock.

71. **Answer: D. Grace Church in Vineyard Haven on Fridays** - All the options are good but, Grace Church Lobster Rolls are for a good cause. And, when you request your Lobster Roll in a container you get twice as much lobster meat with two rolls with a bag of chips for the same price. A must share "islander-insider" tip.

72. **Answer: B. Twenty-two** - The most inspiring way to experience the island is by exploring the various hiking trails provided by Sheriff's Meadow Foundation. With twenty-two different trails throughout the island, you will see the prettiest parts of Noepe. Definitively bring the camera and fluids. Dogs are welcomed on a leash.

73. **Answer: D. Never, ever, ever, ever rent or use a moped on the Vineyard.** The Vineyard is a small island with some very narrow roads with little to no shoulder on most streets. The mopeds max out at 30 mph, which present dangers when speed limits on island reach 45 mph. Someone dies every year riding mopeds. Don't be a statistic!

74. **Answer: D. All of the above** - Ok, this was a gimme. But a "go to" for the kids is a must for any parents' toolbelt.

75. **Answer: A. Edgartown and Oak Bluffs** - Most sit-down restaurants on the island offer cocktails, but only Oak Bluffs and

Edgartown have bars that do not require the patron to purchase food with alcohol.

76. **Answer: D. Edward Brooke** -The former Attorney General for Massachusetts, who went on to be a US Senator for the Commonwealth, and a former boyfriend of Barbara Walters was a Republican who co-wrote *The Civil-Rights Act of 1968*. He was a long-time island resident until his death.

77. **Answer: C. The Shenandoah and The Alabama** - The Original Black Dog Restaurant was started in 1973 to help pay for regular maintenance needed for The Shenandoah - the ship with the blue hull. The restaurant started to sell hats and t-shirts and boom. Who knew a dog could fly. The success led to the purchase of the Alabama – the ship with the white hull. Sunset cruises are offered daily.

78. **Answer: C. Robert Douglas** - Captain Douglas was the only skipper for the Shenandoah, which he designed and built in 1964. The 108-foot top-sail schooner is the largest square-rigged tall ship of its size in the world.

79. **Answer: B. The Alice S. Wentworth** - Purchased in 1921 and sailed until 1943, the Alice S. Wentworth was built in South Norwalk, Connecticut, in 1863. After Zeb retired, the Alice S. Wentworth continued to sail as a Maine windjammer until 1962. She was sold for conversion to a restaurant in 1965 but sank at the dock and finally broke apart in a winter storm in 1974.

80. **Answer: D. All of the above** - All these restaurants offer beautiful water views. But the Lookout Tavern provides an unobstructed view of the Vineyard Sound, while Nancy's and the Atlantic give graceful marina views to set the relaxed island vibe.

81. **Answer: A. Oak Bluff and Vineyard Haven** - All trails on island allow pets on a leash but, Oak Bluffs has a dog park called

Trade Winds and Vineyard Haven has a Dog Park off Holmes' Hole Road for dog social interaction.)

82. **Answer: C. The church was built prior to the existence of the neighboring homes** - Built in 1828 and still used by the oldest practicing congregation on island. It faces Main Street and once had an unobstructed view to the main street before the neighbors moved in.

83. **Answer: B. Polly Hill** - She experimented with the best plants from around the world to selectively present her amazing collection in this garden. It takes the visitors on a whole new experience. Check out the Japanese Puzzle Tree and Dogwood Alley at the Polly Hill Arboretum on State Road in West Tisbury. It's right next to Ag Hall.

84. **Answer: C. The Loft** -This open space Nightclub & Concert venue with a large dance floor also doubles as a pool hall with darts, shuffle board, Jingo and other adult games. It often features well-known, current, and past musical acts, along with showcasing a DJ on other nights.

85. **Answer: C. Island Alpaca Company** - The alpaca farm only provides clothing made from the alpaca. The Allen Farm pro-vides clothing made from sheep and offers fresh lamb meat. It is also a favorite spot for wedding receptions because of its gor-geous view of the Atlantic Ocean. The remaining two offer fresh produce and have websites for pre-orders and delivery.

86. **Answer: B. Your Taxi** - Another "islander-insider" tip; it's not the prettiest but it is the cheapest transportation on island. Cabs charge by the town and the number of towns you may or may not have to cross to get to your destination. Your Taxi's rates start at $10.00.

87. **Answer: E. R & B Eatery in Edgartown** - 7a breakfast sand-wiches, lunch specials are unmatched. Black Sheep Mercantile's

specialty sandwiches and entrees stand alone. Menemsha offers specialty entrees and sandwiches that can't be touched. The Chilmark General Store has it all including great pizza, outrageous salads, and daily specials. Always have your camera on the ready, this is "celebrity central" because most celebrities live up-island and CGM is the only market in the area.

88. **Answer: A. 200 pieces of silver** (Mayhew got a package deal of a lifetime.)

89. **Answer: A. True** - Tony's Market offers great sides and even better entrees. Stay away from the Reuben, but jump on the meatballs. Fat Ronnie Burgers is the second-best late-night treat. Enjoy the killer fries or O-rings, as you build your own burger.

90. **Answer: C. Long Point Beach** - Though Long Point is my second-favorite beach on the entire island after Lucy Vincent Beach, it is only accessible by car. In addition, there is a fixed number of parking spots and a parking fee, so the beach is never crowded. But it's not unusual to see a line of cars waiting for parking. Like Long Point Beach, Lucy Vincent and South Beach have large waves because the body of water is the Atlantic Ocean. Fuller Beach and State Beach have docile waves and are more family-friendly and ideal for the little ones. The body of water for these beaches is the Vineyard Sound, which is the water between the mainland and the island. All four beaches are easily accessible by one or two buses. Daily bus passes are $8.00 daily or $1.25 per town.

91. **Answer: E. Cannonball Park in Edgartown** - Though it's a beautiful memorial park to the soldiers of the Civil War that is highlighted by several cannons on the edges of the park, there is no restroom. The rest of the locations are good to have in your hip pocket.

92. **Answer: B. Dr. Henry Louis Gates** - The "Finding Your Roots" host is an island mainstay during the summer months and he

loves to chat in general. He hosts a multi-day symposium every year in August. The panel discussions always consist of the elite in finance, politics and social issues.

93. **Answer: B. & D. Offshore Ale Brew Pub and Mad Martha's Farmers Brewery** - Both pubs offer food and micro-beer brewed on the premises. Offshore Ale has some of the best bar pies on the island, along with the best selection of oysters and fish & chips down island. Another unique feature, the huge barrel of peanuts at the door. Beer and wine only but, all the peanuts' shells can go on the floor with the sawdust. One of the most distinctive interiors on island, both are casual dining.

94. **Answer: A. True** - Along with the multiple bike paths down-island (Edgartown, Oak Bluffs and Vineyard Haven), all of the VTA buses have bike racks which hold up to three bikes. In addition, during the summer months the Menemsha Bike Ferry takes bikes and their riders to and from Lobsterville Beach in Aquinnah. Bike rentals are in every town.

95. **Answer: C. Early Visitors to the island mistook the multiple beach plum bushes for grapes on the vine or bush** - Used to make jam, jelly, pies and pastries beach plums are large dark purple fruit that really resembles large grapes. They were once a common sight along barrier beaches and coastal regions from the mid-Atlantic states to the maritime provinces of Canada. An unfortunate consequence of coastal development is the marked decline of this lovely plant that is now listed as rare in Northeastern coastal states. But, on the Vineyard they grow like dandelions near beach areas.

96. **Answer: B. The Orange Peel Bakery** - Another "islander-insider" tip; The Orange Peel is a true representation of "the island vibe". This bakery is owned and operated by Wampanoag Tribal member Juli Vanderhoop. It offers an array of baked goods and treats, along with its annex establishment located at the Gay Head cliffs. Since the bakery is often unstaffed, it operates on the

honor system by requesting customers place payment in a locked steel box. That's a beautiful thing.

Juli describes Pizza Night as follows, "Pizza Night at the Orange Peel Bakery happens nine months a year, from April to November. Orange Peel Bakery is all about community. It might look like a private party, but don't let that dissuade you-it's not. Walk right up, say hello, and ease into the scene. No dogs please! PIZZA NIGHT IS OFFERING A SHORT MENU OF PIZZA TO CHOOSE FROM. PIZZA'S ARE 12 INCHES AND YOU CAN CHOOSE TO HANG OUT OR GET IT TO GO! BYOB!"

It is located on State Road on the left side after the Wampanoag Tribe entrance. Seating is set-up outside with picnic tables, acoustic musical performers, wonderfully kind people, families, locals, "wash-a-shores", vacationers and seasonal residents. Have the camera ready. The celebrity island residents love this event. It allows them to interact with people as everyday people. They can be "just another Bozo on the island."

97. **Answer: D. The Depot Market** - The remaining choice offers specialty coffee options and pastries.

98. **ANSWER: G. All of the above** - The Black Dog: best hash, the most pancake variety, and outstanding lunch menu; The Art Cliff Diner: Everything, especially the French Toast, Linda Jean's: great omelets, terrific home-fries and breakfast; The Plane View Diner has it all for breakfast and lunch in a simple setting with a super view of the planes; The Waterside Market: specialty lunch menu and breakfast sandwiches make it sparkle. No bad choices on this list.

99. **Answer: B, C, D, E** ("If you're gonna be a bear… be a grizzly" and get ready to say yummy.)

100. **Answer: A. Backdoor Donuts** - The apple fritters and Apple Cider Donuts are so good, that even the Obamas' daughters can be seen waiting in line.

101. **Answer: H. Sharky's Cantina on Circuit Avenue, Oak Bluffs** (All of the other choices are top notch with great wine selections.)

102. **Answer: A. Rev. Thomas Mayhew wanted to gain favor of the Duke of York, so he named the town after The Duke of York's son Edgar** - It is the only Edgartown in the world and the oldest town on the island. Its architecture for the majority of the homes is colonial base with Greek influence reflected in large columns in the front of the structure. The town's overall presentation is of an Old Whaling Town. In contrast, Oak Bluffs architecture is Victorian influenced.

All businesses referenced in this trivia questionnaire have their own websites for additional information.

Martha's Vineyard, Cape Cod, Massachusetts

Photo Questions & Answers

1. **Where is this lighthouse located?**

2. **What is the name of this church and where is it located?**

3. **Where did the name Telegraph Hill originate?**

4. **What is the name of this hotel?**

5. What is the name and location of this airport?

6. What architectural style is this house and where is this style of building most prevalent?

7. **What style is this house and where is it located?**

8. **Where is this sign located?**

9. **What is this building and where is it located?**

10. **What is the sculpture and where is it?**

11.   At what intersection are these signs located?

12.   What is the name of this public golf course and where is it?

13. This is Town Beach in Oak Bluffs. What is another name for it?

14. This beach is known for its big waves. What is it name?

15. What is this building and where it is located?

16. This ferry is docked at which town? What is the ferry's name?

17. The West Tisbury Farmers' Markets and Vineyard Artisan Festivals are held here. What is this building?

18. The West Tisbury Town Hall was originally built for what purpose?

19.   This bell, which called children of Dukes County Academy to class from 1847 to 1924, is located in which town?

20.   What is the name of the lighthouse off in the distance?

21. **According to legend, why are the cliffs of Aquinnah red?**

Photo Answers

1. West Chop

2. The Old Whaling Church in Edgartown

3. Starting in 1801, a semaphore system carried messages 75 miles in 10 minutes between Edgartown and Boston. Operators were stationed in towers on top of the telegraph hills so signals could be transmitted. Their purpose: to communicate news and instructions between ship owners and ship captains. Today, telegraph hills stand in Edgartown, Woods Hole, Sandwich, Plymouth, Duxbury, Hull, Provincetown and South Boston, all in Massachusetts.

4. Harbor View Hotel in Edgartown

5. Katama Airpark Edgartown

6. It is Carpenter Gothic style, most popular in the Campgrounds in Oak Bluffs.

7. Greek revival style was most popular with whaling captains. This house overlooks Edgartown Harbor.

8. In the garden behind the Martha's Vineyard Museum.

9. Martha's Vineyard Museum in Vineyard Haven

10. Harpooner located in Menemsha, Chilmark.

11. At the intersection of State Road and West Tisbury-Edgartown Rd. in Vineyard Haven.

12. Pink Meadows Golf Club, 320 Golf Club Rd, Vineyard Haven

13. Inkwell Beach

14. South Beach

15. The Nathen Mayhew Schoolhouse was built in 1828 as a one room school house. The Daughters of the American Revolution operated a maritime museum there for many years. It is part of the Vineyard Reservation Trust.

16. The Martha's Vineyard Eagle docks in Vineyard Haven.

17. Constructed by the Martha's Vineyard Agricultural Society at the crossroads of the island, the Grange Hall in West Tisbury is the center of agriculture and commerce for the Vineyard. The grand post and beam barn stands as an enduring landmark and serves as a gathering place for farmers, artisans, and residents. Granges have been the heart of rural American communities for generations. The home of local chapters of the Order of Patrons of Husbandry, Grange Halls are where farmers have traditionally gathered to learn new agricultural practices, develop strategic business partnerships, and barter for goods and services. Grange Halls also serve as a gathering place for community celebrations and annual agricultural fairs. In 1858 the Martha's Vineyard Agricultural Society was created and held its first Fair.

18. The West Tisbury Town Hall, built in 1858, was the first schoolhouse on the island.

19. It is located in West Tisbury on the grounds of the Town Hall.

20. The Gay Head Lighthouse in Aquinnah.

21. From near the entrance to his den on the Aquinnah Cliffs, Moshup would wade into the ocean, pick up a whale, fling it against the Cliffs to kill it, and then cook it over the fire that burned continually. The blood from these whales stained the clay banks of the Cliffs dark red.